Empowering the Congregational Nurse

Implementing a Faith Community Nursing Practice

A Self-Study Course

By

Linda Royer, RN, PhD

Affiliated in an Imaginary Way with

Connections of Hope
123 Sunrise Drive
Anytown, U.S.A.

2019

FOREWARD

Society is at the nexus of economic instability and debt burden, inadequate planning for health and for healthcare services, aging health professional workforces, increasing immigration, job losses, rising healthcare costs, uncertain insurance coverage putting individuals and families at risk for catastrophic illness or injury, emerging infectious diseases, and natural and man-made accidents and disasters. Working from "upstream" is a wise strategy, which is where nurses wish to be. However, Community Health nurses (CHN) are challenged by budget constraints and diminishing workforce capacity to optimally perform their core functions of surveillance, assurance of care, and health promotion. They need assistance from their colleagues in the community who are potential partnering nurses. This collaboration is key to bringing about seamless health care delivery for now and the future.

Many configurations of collaboration now exist, such as health care teams of physician-nurse-patient-therapists-pharmacist and family. Community human service agencies partner with industry or non-profit volunteer organizations. Partnerships between universities and health and human service agencies are proliferating as outcomes demonstrate improved access to care and reduction of morbidity and mortality. It is time all nurses in all specialties, active or inactive, young graduates or retired consider ways they can effect collaborative relationships in their communities with other nurses and health professionals to bring health promotion and health care to their neighbors and community members. The purpose of this "Empowering the Nurse Leader" bundle of resources is to illustrate how the nurse in the faith community may be a catalyst of small and larger community efforts.

In *Crossing the Quality Chasm: A New Health System for the 21st Century,* the Institute of Medicine (2001) recommended that comprehensive healthcare reform should achieve 6 national quality aims: "safety, effectiveness, patient-centeredness, timeliness, efficiency, and equity." Subsequent to that report, the IOM in 2003 convened a multidisciplinary summit to examine the education of health professionals and make recommendations that would bridge the chasm to quality. Five core competencies within and across the professions of nursing, medicine, pharmacy and allied health were selected: (1) provide patient-centered care, (2) work effectively in interdisciplinary teams, (3) employ evidence-based practice, (4) apply quality improvement, and (5) utilize informatics. O'Neil of the California-based Center for Health Professions recommended earlier in 1998 that, among 5 goals, two are supportive to the purpose of this idea: (1) focusing on population-based health-and specifically behavioral health within it-and (2) creating strategic partnerships.

Because there is interest in the community aspects of all patient care, Baldwin, Conger, Abegglen & Hill (1998) contended that population focus should permeate all levels of nursing practice and emanate from the baccalaureate level. Emphasis in practice should be on health promotion and disease and injury prevention. Population-focused nursing also connotes competent cultural practice that seeks to understand and celebrate the differences in individuals and their social patterns as well as assuring that culturally diverse professionals are recruited into service. To serve the professional needs of nurses and other providers, *Competencies for Population Health Professions* (2019) have been developed to exact quality care in assessment of needs. You may find them at www.phf.org/resoucetools/pages/core_public_health_competencies.aspx.

What a time for nursing! Nurses have the knowledge, skills, and willingness to intervene for quality of life. We are in great demand! Diligent efforts of nursing leaders, practitioners, educators, and students have increased the awareness of the value of nurses among the public, legislators, and health care leaders. In the face of opportunity, there are obstacles in our path: (1) a decreasing capacity (faculty) and space for educating nurses—leading to fewer licensure candidates, (2) aging of the nursing workforce with impending retirement (average age 47 years), (3) only a modest return of inactive nurses to the workforce, (4) a turnover rate of 17%. Alarmingly, a demand for more than 1 million new and replacement nurses by 2012 (AACN and HRSA, 2011) was predicted. Now we are in 2019 and the demand will increase.

Conditions in the nursing workforce only reflect what is occurring in most health care professions. Demographic changes in society present an ever-increasing challenge to the health of the nation and the globe. In the IOM report (2008), "Retooling for an Aging America: Building the Health Care Workforce," this statement summarized current conditions in the healthcare workforce: ". . . as the population of seniors grows to comprise approximately 20 percent of the U.S. population, they will face a health care workforce that is too small and critically unprepared to meet their health needs." The committee concluded that if our aging family members and friends are to continue to live robustly and in the best possible health, "we need bold initiatives designed to:

•explore ways to broaden the duties and responsibilities of workers at various levels of training;
•better prepare informal caregivers to tend to the needs of aging family members and friends;
•develop new models of health care delivery and payment as old ways sponsored by federal programs such as Medicare prove to be ineffective and inefficient."

In the 2010 IOM report, "The Future of Nursing: Leading Change, Advancing Health," a Robert Wood Johnson Foundation-supported committee chaired by Donna Shalala in the Institute of Medicine, summarized its response to the expectations of the newly-signed Affordable Care Act with this statement:

"This report begins with the assumption that nursing can fill such new and expanded roles in a redesigned health care system. To take advantage of these opportunities, however, nurses must be allowed to practice in accordance with their professional training, and the education they receive must better prepare them to deliver patient-centered, equitable, safe, high-quality healthcare services; engage with physicians and other health care professionals to deliver efficient and effective care; and assume leadership roles in the redesign of the health care system. In particular, we believe the search for an expanded workforce to serve the millions who will now have access to health insurance for the first time will require changes in nursing scopes of practice, advances in the education of nurses across all levels, improvements in the practice of nursing across the continuum of care, transformation in the utilization of nurses across settings, and leadership at all levels so nurses can be deployed effectively and appropriately as partners in the health care team."

Our marching orders are laid out for us, nurses: capitalize on caring, on collaboration, on leadership skill-building, on continuity, on innovation. We live in a globalized society. With the shattering of our nation's relative isolation and perceived invincibility, we not only lead in health-related interventions, we share in the world's woes such as terrorism and rapid transmission of disease, and we see our complexion changing with an increasing stream of several migrating populations. We face significant challenges. And now we, as a country, are reforming health care delivery. The nursing profession has been preparing for perceived changes to come and trying to imagine what is not yet clear. We are somewhat hampered by our past—the way it has been done, what has worked before. O'Neil states, "We do not have any natural ways of thinking about the entire community when it comes to health and health care. Even public health has been segmented in its work over the past few decades. The health care reform provides an opportunity to think expansively and inclusively about what people need and what keeps them healthy. The real promise of this epochal change won't be realized without such reflection and action."

So, the door is open to nurses in the community to create care delivery systems that work. Faith communities reach many individuals in need of education about health and prevention, of consultation about health concerns, of physical assistance, of chronic disease or disability management. This practice-building bundle of resources is designed to aid the "called" professional servant to a unique service for communities already committed to the ministry of Christ in making man "whole."

How to Use These Resources

You have in this 2-volume "e-book bundle" a general guide to empower you as the leader of nurse-initiated health ministries practice. It is written specifically to an audience of Christian nurses; however, the principles within are applicable to most communities of faith. As you examine the Table of Contents you will see there are 12 chapters in this volume that lead you from the inception of an idea to build a congregational nurse practice in one faith community through logical steps toward establishing it. Stakeholder recruitment strategies, program and services planning, and training of volunteers follow. Much time is given to the role and functions of the nurse in the congregation. Finally, interaction with the community at large is discussed. The references for each chapter follow Chapter 12. Many excellent sources are there. Among the Appendices you will find working documents, practice models, a strategic plan example, stories of nurses in the role, and more. **PowerPoint presentations** are at the end of this volume.

The major companion volume in this "bundle" is an Operations Manual for an imagined interfaith consortium organization called **"Connections of Hope."** It is assumed that, after a congregational nurse establishes his/her practice in their own faith community, there will be a desire to link with other like communities and even with those of various faiths to better serve the needs of especially vulnerable populations of the region. So the **"Connections of Hope"** Operations Manual describes the activities of the consortium. Often this volume you hold, **"Empowering the Congregational Nurse"**, refers to guidelines in the Operations Manual.

In the Operations Manual much attention is focused on how to manage the practice and the documents, procedures, personnel, and structure necessary for it. There you will find explicit guidelines for recruitment and management of volunteers. Liability issues are addressed. Finally, organizational evaluation is discussed. Again, there are several practical resources in the Appendices.

My prayer is that this "bundle" will serve you well on your adventure. We know efforts of ministry are not done in isolation nor of our impoverished power, but with God. In Isaiah 41:13 He says,

"For I am the Lord, your God, who takes hold of your right hand and says to you,

'Do not fear; I will help you.'"

TABLE OF CONTENTS

Chapter One

Define the terms and operationalize concepts of health, community health and a "healthy community"

OBJECTIVES

1. Define, identify, and describe dimensions of a healthy community
2. Explain wholistic determinants of health in the context of current concerns
3. Interpret theoretical principles of responsibility toward healthy communities
4. Describe at least six techniques or instruments for gathering assessment data
5. Suggest ways assessment data would influence development of a congregational nurse program
6. Explain through theory and application the importance of skillful work with families and groups
7. Describe possible community partnerships utilizing a systems approach and referencing national and professional indicator and standard tools.

CONTEXT

A. Definition from WHO and others. Your definition . . .

- World Health Organization's definition of <u>health</u>: "Health is a state of physical, mental and social well-being and the ability to function and not merely the absence of illness and infirmity."

- Health is not just the absence of disease, but a balanced state of well-being resulting from harmonious interaction of body, mind, and spirit.

- Well-being can realistically be considered as a point along the health-illness continuum, reflecting one's current state of being at approximately 4 stages: 1) clinical health or the absence of disease, 2) one's role performance health or the ability to perform one's social roles satisfactorily, 3) one's adaptiveness to circumstances and the environment, and 4) eudaemonistic health, or self-actualization and the attainment of one's greatest human potential/personal best.

- Because it is subjective, we must personally determine our state of health based on what we know, how we feel, whether we are able to meet reasonable expectations of society, and whether we are satisfied with our quality of life.

B. Define Community
Community is defined in many ways: by function--meeting mutual needs interdependently; by locality; or the existence of commonalities among its members. Critical attributes of communities are: 1) group orientation, 2) the bond between individuals, 3) human interaction (which may lead to a bond).

- A working definition I like is: A community is a group of people who share some type of bond, who interact with each other, and who function collectively regarding common concerns.

Community health, then, is the focus of health professionals on the biopsychosocial needs of aggregates of the community who have formed bonds either territorially or relationally recognizing that personal troubles of individuals become societal issues; by extension, community health is competence in carrying out responsibilities to the health of the community.

A healthy community therefore is an aggregate group, neighborhood, town, city, county, etc. that maintains as its goal: seeking quality of life for its members through adequate health and social services, transportation, food and water sources, employment, recreation, education, shelter, spiritual resources, and social opportunities.

More Resources:

View PowerPoint presentation "Community as Recipient of Your Care" in Presentations in back of this volume.
Article "A Model for the Delivery of Culturally Competent Community Care" by Kim-Godwin, Yeoun Soo PhD RN MPH; Clarke, Pamela N. PhD RN MPH; Barton, Leslie BA, in *Journal of Advanced Nursing (35)* 6, September 2001 pp 918-925.

C. Characterize a "spiritual community"
One could consider the community of the early church in apostolic times (The Biblical Book of Acts) and their continual spiritual practices of worship and reminiscent conversation as well as their care for each other in times of political and religious oppression. Today, we think of a congregational community where members meet regularly to worship God and fellowship. The spiritual "glue" is the love and disinterested benevolence among the members and toward the stranger near and far from their door.

What are your thoughts?

D. Determinants of health: perceived by health professionals and perceived by various population groups (those with chronic disease, the disabled, marginalized people, those with depression, etc.).
Healthcare leaders in the U.S. use carefully researched marks called determinants by which to identify health concerns and risks to health. By referencing these, benchmarks can be established for health care agencies and a determination can be made of improvement in health of populations. Healthy People 2020 indicators from 12 health concerns (topics) have produced 24 objectives based on 12 indicators which apply to all of nursing practice. They encompass:

•The Biological and Behavioral nature of the Individual

•The Social environment (relationships in the home and the community)

•The Physical Environment

•Policies and Interventions directed toward people and their state of health

•Access to quality health care

To carry that a step further in order to make health care delivery more relevant to congregational nursing, wholistic (Whole Person) determinants of health may fall in the following categories:
1. Coping & Adaptation toward Stress
How one responds to natural and man-made stressors, revealed by attitudes expressed, management of time and priorities of life, and nutritional and activity practices.

2. Spiritual Relationships

People are at their best when living for others. We need the vertical connection with our Creator to obtain the tools and skills to develop healthy and satisfying horizontal friendships with others in our sphere of living. Appreciation for things created bring peace and contentment to our lives.

3. Family Relationships

Understanding the dynamics and communication patterns used among family members while learning about the roles and functions of each member helps us to perpetuate healthy relationships throughout society. A strong relationship with the Heavenly Family increases that of the earthly family.

4. Nutrition & Water

Adherence to the principles of balanced nutrition based on inherent body needs and expenditures and the use of adequate quantities of pure water for internal hydration and external hygiene supports a healthy lifestyle.

5. Exercise & Motion

Activities that include stretching, muscle development, and aerobic motion lead to a balanced, wholistic lifestyle, reduces stress, and enhances enjoyment of a healthy lifestyle.

6. Pleasure-seeking activities

Mind-altering agents such as tobacco, marijuana, alcohol, illegal drugs, and some over-the-counter medications promote an unnatural, habituated (slavish), and physically detrimental lifestyle. A myriad of research studies reveal the decline of sub-populations of society who indulge in them. Overuse and dependence on prescription drugs to the exclusion of behavior modifications are also at fault.

7. Personal Risk Management

Risk is defined as vulnerability to injury/disease. We put ourselves "at risk" by exposing our bodies/minds to hazards that may cause injury or disease or even death. Attitudes and the resultant choices we make position us for well being or risk. It is important to individuals who desire to control (with their Spiritual God) their lives that management of activities which avoid risk of exposure be primary when making life choices.

8. Achievement

Reaching personal goals, or as Maslow puts it, "self-actualization", employs self-improvement measures and evaluation of choices, continued education, practiced motivation, and over-all, a sense of the "whole picture" or global view. Including spiritual components to this global thinking enhances ones understanding of purpose in living among the society of other earth inhabitants.

From a national viewpoint current community health issues are: (Refer to MedicineNet.com)

- HIV/AIDS
- violence (domestic and at the community and global levels)
- threat of terrorist acts and disaster preparedness
- emergence of and rapidly-introduced infectious diseases
- obesity
- chronic disease

•substance use and abuse

•motor vehicle accidents and unintentional injury.

You can probably think of more.

E. Creating Health in unfavorable circumstances

This is the challenge to Congregational Nurses, who are truly Community Health Nurses. Being privileged to visit with individuals and families in their homes as opposed to in fellowship at the church reveals the true circumstances in which people live daily. It is here that unfavorable circumstances may be observed and where the caring and diplomatic skills of the "health visitor" are demonstrated. To the extent of permission from the individual served and the maintenance of safety, a wholistic environment conducive to health and quality of life is facilitated.

[Refer to the presentation "Vulnerable Populations"]

F. The Conservation Principles - Levine

As stewards of this earth, we can place a particular significance on Myra Levine's Conservation Principles. They are focused on conservation of the person's wholeness and testify to the nurse's activity based on appreciation for one's integrity. The principles are: 1) Energy, 2) Structural Integrity--the ability of the body to repair itself in the event of injury, 3) Personal Integrity--recognition of the self, 4) Social Integrity. Before her death in 1996, she elaborated on Adaptation, one's reciprocal interaction with the environment, as being the bridge from one reality to another. The diversity of our genetic inheritance from earth's previous generations provides the ability to adapt to changing conditions. Levine also referred to Gen. 1:27 where the creation of Man is described and emphasizes the sanctity of life, which spills over into the recognition of social integrity. [You may read more about this in Jacqueline Fawcett's *Analysis and Evaluation of Contemporary Nursing Knowledge* (2000), F.A. Davis Publishers.

G. Measurement instruments and techniques; content validity

The following instruments may be found in Public Health texts and through internet searches. They are reliable and validated tools to ascertain significant information about individual and aggregate health status.

1. Medical Outcomes Study-36 - The Medical Model.
2. Quality of Life Index. Refer to Dr. Carol Farren webpage
3. High-level Wellness or Wellness Model of Health Refer to a history sketch and intended meaning by the originator of the concept, Dr. Halbert Dunn at www.wwu.edu.
4. Social support and caring scales

   a. Duke-UNC Functional Questionnaire for Senior Adults

   b. MOS Social Support Survey, researched by the RAND Corp and School of Nursing at UCSF

5. Well-Being Assessments:

   a. Ryff's Psychological Well-Being Scale—an 84-item validated instrument built on 6 scales: Self-Acceptance, Positive Relations with Others, Autonomy, Environment Mastery, Purpose in Life, and Personal Growth. You may obtain it by email request to Dr. Carol Ryff at cryff@wisc.edu.

b. Jarel's Spiritual Well-being Scale—a 21-item instrument based on 3 dimensions: Faith/Belief, Self Responsibility, and Life Satisfaction. It may be obtained from Marquette University's College of Nursing, Phone - 414.288.3800.

c. Gallup's "Well-Being: The 5 Essential Elements" by Rath and Harter (2010), available in print and as a Kindle™ electronic document for less than $15. It is a report on a landmark study of people in 150 countries surveyed about their perceptions of five universal and interconnected elements that shape their lives: Career, social, financial, physical, and community well-being.

d. Surgeon General's Family Health History. Similar tools may be found at the CDC website .

H. *National Benchmarks and Standards*
All community health nurses should be familiar with sources of national data, practice standards, health promotion guidelines, and legislative activities to guide the development and maintenance of a congregational nursing service. A few of high priority are listed below.

•*Healthy People 2010 & 2020:* The national progress indicator

•*Community Health Status Indicators* – Notice county health rankings

•*National Public Health Performance Standards* – Conduct you can expect from the U.S.   Public Health Service and its employees in various disciplines.

•*Core Competencies of Public/Community Health Nurses* – Specific skills and responses citizens should expect from P/CHNs according to their levels of preparation.

•*Turning Point > Accreditation > Quality Improvements* – Goals and accomplishments in this past decade of the movement toward quality of service by Public Health organizations as accreditation is achieved.

NOTES . . .

Chapter Two

GOAL:
Define the terms and operationalize concepts of health promotion and self care

OBJECTIVES

1. Describe and explain three types of theories that characterize motivation to change behavior.
2. Explain why motivating individuals to change behavior is a primary role in community nursing and how ethical principles in nursing guide practice.
3. Interpret selected learning concepts and describe learner responses.
4. Characterize the effective educator.

CONTENT

In this chapter terms and concepts of health, and particularly of nursing, will be reviewed in order to enhance your knowledge and perceptions of individual and aggregate needs in your faith community and, by extension, the community at large. Links to resources that provide concept illustrations, applications to practice, enlargement of meaning will guide your journey. Key points about health behaviors and lifestyle change are as follows:

A. Motivating individuals to change behavior-a primary role in the community
Health is the opposite of illness role behavior where one acts on symptoms of illness to discover a suitable remedy, or sick role behavior where one tries to facilitate recovery from illness or maintains a dependency on others for mediation or treatment.

Health behavior can be described as self-defined behaviors of a broad scope of practice that are performed to protect against disease and to promote a higher level of health or quality of life. It may not be observable because it may be mental events (decisions) and feeling states (peace and contentment). It may encompass personal attributes such as health beliefs, values, expectations, motives, perceptions, and personality characteristics.
Example: Getting immunized against Hepatitis B or exercising regularly to maintain cardiovascular health in the face of family history of chronic disease.

•Health promotion behavior is behavior directed toward achieving a greater level of health and well-being.
Example: Exercising regularly because it makes one feel energetic and able to function at a higher level.

•Illness/disease prevention is behavior directed toward reducing the threat of illness, injury, disease, or complications.
Example: Wearing a seat belt, helmet, protective gear when engaging in risk activity in car, bicycle, or roller blades; participating in the immunization schedule for family members.

•Health maintenance behavior is directed toward keeping a current state of health and well-being.
Example: Exercising to maintain ideal weight, taking Vitamin E to keep immune system strong.

These indicate that behavior can be determined according to the performance choices one makes.

<u>Leading to Self-care.</u>   Here individuals make their own choices and perform activities on their own behalf to maintain life, health, and well-being and to improve illness states. To do this they need to be informed. Health professionals facilitate this activity.

All through recorded history human behavior has reflected both a glimpse of the estimate of one's personal worth and the beliefs and values of one's community at the time. What perplexes self-determined individuals is the health-negating behaviors of those who make deleterious choices that not only affect themselves, but reaches into the family and the community in which they live and eventually around the world. Today we see the results of such choices causing at least half of all premature deaths in our nation-a staggering burden for society. And if we examine the status of world health we see some countries spiraling down into serious decline on their current course.

<u>The Whole Person.</u>   Fundamentally, a person is a whole being when conceptualized as a composite of physical forces (neurobiochemical), mental-emotional energies (biopsychosocial), and spiritual dimension. All of these elements are integrated and interwoven into a whole human being. Some describe the whole person experience as a spiraling course through time and space from conception to infinity. That is the objective view, as one outside looking in. In the personal human experience of a believer in the power of our Creator and the saving grace of Christ, it may mean enjoying a life-sustaining relationship with Him and feeling confident and at peace in whatever circumstances, knowing you are living a lifestyle that honors Him. It may mean that the "solid self" is more than being actualized through values clarification and consistency of beliefs, feelings, and resultant actions. You are capable of seeing others, including the unlovely, through the eyes of Christ and of actually becoming a conduit for the expression of His love and concern for all humanity. This pattern of living transcends self-actualization and reaches into the realms of Heaven.

<u>Moral Development.</u> Historic studies in Moral Development and its impact on learning and character were conducted by Jean Piaget, Lawrence Kohlberg, Elliot Turiel, and Carol Gilligan. A synopsis of their work can be viewed at http://tigger.uic.edu/~lnucci/MoralEd/overviewtext.html . From that article I shall refer discussion here to Kohlberg, who offers an understanding of the process in 6 stages.

"On the basis of his research, Kohlberg identified six stages of moral reasoning grouped into three major levels. Each level represented a fundamental shift in the social-moral perspective of the individual. At the first level, the preconventional level, a person's moral judgments are characterized by a concrete, individual perspective. Within this level, a Stage 1 heteronomous orientation focuses on avoiding breaking rules that are backed by punishment, obedience for its own sake and avoiding the physical consequences of an action to persons and property. As in Piaget's framework, the reasoning of Stage 1 is characterized by ego-centrism and the inability to consider the perspectives of others. At Stage 2 there is the early emergence of moral reciprocity. The Stage 2 orientation focuses on the instrumental, pragmatic value of an action. Reciprocity is of the form, "you scratch my back and I'll scratch yours." The Golden Rule becomes, "If someone hits you, you hit them back." At Stage 2 one follows the rules only when it is to someone's immediate interests. What is right is what's fair in the sense of an equal exchange, a deal, an agreement. At Stage 2 there is an understanding that everybody has his(her) own interest to pursue and these conflict, so that right is relative (in the concrete individualist sense).

Individuals at the conventional level of reasoning, however, have a basic understanding of conventional morality, and reason with an understanding that norms and conventions are necessary to uphold society. They tend to be self-identified with these rules, and uphold them consistently, viewing morality as acting in accordance with what society defines as right. Within this level, individuals at Stage 3 are aware of shared feelings, agreements, and expectations which take primacy over individual interests. Persons at Stage 3 define what is right in terms of what is expected by people close to one's self, and in terms of the stereotypic roles that define being good - e.g., a good brother, mother, teacher. Being good means keeping mutual relationships, such as trust, loyalty, respect, and gratitude. The perspective is that of the local community or family. There is not as yet a consideration of the generalized social system. Stage 4 marks the shift from defining what is right in terms of local norms and role expectations to defining right in terms of the laws and norms established by the larger social system. This is the "member of society" perspective in which one is moral by fulfilling the actual duties defining one's social responsibilities. One must obey the law except in extreme cases in which the law comes into conflict with other prescribed social duties. Obeying the law is seen as necessary in order to maintain the system of laws which protect everyone.

Finally, the post conventional level is characterized by reasoning based on principles, using a "prior to society" perspective. These individuals reason based on the principles which underlie rules and norms, but reject a uniform application of a rule or norm. While two stages have been presented within the theory, only one, Stage 5, has received substantial empirical support. Stage 6 remains as a theoretical endpoint which rationally follows from the preceding 5 stages. *In essence this last level of moral judgment entails reasoning rooted in the ethical fairness principles from which moral laws would be devised. Laws are evaluated in terms of their coherence with basic principles of fairness rather than upheld simply on the basis of their place within an existing social order.* Thus, there is an understanding that elements of morality such as regard for life and human welfare transcend particular cultures and societies and are to be upheld irrespective of other conventions or normative obligations." Stage 6 describes "reasoning rooted in the ethical fairness principles from which moral laws would be devised. Laws are evaluated in terms of their coherence with basic principles of fairness rather than upheld simply on the basis of their place within an existing social order."

This leads directly to the topic of ethics and how ethical principles influence the work of the congregational nurse.

B. Ethics affecting health
First of all, nurses learn early and practice always under the document of "Code of Ethics for Nursing." In it there are 9 provisions; the first one leads the charge with:

"The nurse, in all professional relationships, practices with compassion and respect for the inherent dignity, worth, and uniqueness of every individual, unrestricted by considerations of social or economic status, personal attributes, or the nature of health problems."

The subsequent provisions address:

- Commitment to those served

- Promoting and advocating for and striving to protect the health, safety, and rights of the patient

- Responsibility and accountability for practice and delegation of tasks with optimum care in mind

•Responsibility to self to preserve integrity, safety, competence and continue personal growth

•Engaging in efforts at improving health care environments and conditions consistent with the values of the profession

•Participating in advancement of the profession

•Collaborating with other health professionals and the public to meet health needs

•As a representative of the profession the nurse promotes community, national, and international efforts to meet health needs.

C. The nature and basis of learning

"Achieving better health is more than turning one's self around or dropping one lifestyle practice considered to be deleterious and picking up better one. It requires more effort subjectively than lapsing into an altered state and awakening to loss of desire at a suggestion. Humans are wired to effect change systematically, in whatever style fits the personality and evolution of character. How we, as health professionals, assist an individual in positive change determines their success to a large proportion. We have the knowledge to impart that effects attitude, practice, and self-efficacy.

Attitude toward making a life change in that how one perceives the message and the messenger's intent gives credibility to the anticipated opportunity and method toward the expected goal.

Practice toward making a life change in that those methodical techniques and the rationale supporting them must be believable, must enhance one's integrity, must be practical, and must be worthy of perpetuating for the remainder of life.

Self-efficacy toward making a life change in that the demeanor of the teacher must communicate a sure power that elicits a self-portrait of belief in envisioned success and self-esteem.

"In this 21st century, the maturational and cultural mix has become complex. Research subjects in behavior change studies are no longer just Caucasian and Black, youth versus adult, male vs. female. A young multitasking, broadly ethnically-diverse, technology-based, well-traveled and communicative, and psychologically-inured generation has emerged. Older adults are now children of the 60s with a skeptical orientation toward lifestyle behavior and results of decades of harmful health practices. Improving their health looms as a formidable option and, in many, futility overwhelms the spirit. Youth and young adults who should have the edge on positive lifestyles assume risk behaviors against their better judgment, influenced by the stresses of society, the political uncertainties, and sometimes the spiritual hopelessness about the future."

The paragraphs above are lifted from another source for aiding individuals in changing health behaviors, **"Transforming Lives to Whole Personhood"**. Visit the whole course at the **Dimensions In Learning** website at http://www.frameworkhealth.org

Here are two suggested activities by which to engage groups in discussion concerning approaches to life changes in health using theories learned above:

•Progressive daisy-chain discussion development wherein a concept is shared with one individual in the group to be taken up by each of the others in turn and built upon until the conclusion is announced to the large group.

•Role playing with the phenomenon of the variety of learning styles (preferences): tactile, cognitive, visual, kinetic.

D. Conceptual models of health; Values and Beliefs

"What It Really Means to be Healthy!" is a health behavior change handbook for health professionals and all interested in health that can be inexpensively purchased at Lulu.com. In it the following concepts and instruments are described. These are concepts common to nursing literature and utilized in part or in whole in every-day practice. They help us to understand response patterns of the learner; barriers to change; compliance; literacy.

•Health Belief Model

•Health Promotion Model

•Self-Care; Self-care rooted in spirituality

•Psychoneuroimmunology and healthy lifestyle

I encourage you to follow the rapidly-growing knowledge in brain science as it relates to learning and behavior. Couple that with new understandings of the results of traumatic brain injury. Soldiers returning from the battlefields are and will be integrating into society, some with latent signs of injury, some after rehabilitation. You may find them in your community of service. It is important that you can assess their needs, participate in their recovery or refer them to appropriate therapists, and facilitate their integration into the family of faith.

Health Literacy is a concern among health leaders because there are so many avenues by which to receive information about health, medical conditions, and self-improvement. As a nurse leader you are daily placed in the position of teaching or directing individuals to reliable information. Health literacy is defined in application terms on www.Health.gov in a fact sheet guide. There are 3 articles online at the ANA website I encourage you to read on this topic. They are:

Information Resources: The Digital Divide: How Wide and How Deep?
posted: 8/30/2008 1:05:45 PM [html]

Understanding Cultural and Linguistic Barriers to Health Literacy
posted: 7/21/2010 3:17:27 PM [html]

Information Resources: Information Literacy: The Benefits of Partnership
posted: 2/5/2009 2:26:37 PM [html]

E. The effective educator

I will give you some examples of my philosophy toward teaching and the field of education.

Here are ten guiding principles to knowledge and future learning that have been proposed by Allan Ornstein (1998) which lead to my personal philosophical leaning:

1. Knowledge begins with the basic tools—the 3 R's and computer literacy

2. Knowledge should facilitate the method of learning by allowing students to assume responsibility for their learning

3. Knowledge should reflect the real world

4. Knowledge should be wholistic and facilitate the development of self-system thinking

5. Knowledge should be applied in a variety of forms and methods to meet varying learning styles

6. Knowledge should prepare the student for utilization of technology

7. Knowledge should prepare the student for the social organization of bureaucracy

8. Knowledge should permit and expect the student to retrieve previously learned knowledge and to process it into more complex form

9. An attitude should be promoted of a lifelong learning quest

10. Knowledge should be taught in the context of values and the promotion of vision, or futuristic insight

 A Christian nurse demonstrates an appreciation for the needs of the vulnerable in their present state while maintaining a futuristic world view of what they can become through the interventions of health care and the power of God. It is gratifying to hold to a belief that recognizes the needs of a contemporary society while anticipating the advent of the coming of Jesus, who will eradicate sin and restore the world to Edenic perfection. As a participant in the sacred work of refreshing (Psalms 23), repairing (Isaiah 58), and restoring (2 Kings 5; Isaiah 38:16; Revelation 22), the nurse, as a change agent, holds in his/her hands the destiny of those served. She knows that through (1) love, (2) respect for the whole person, (3) a wholistic approach to healing, and (4) equity that allows personal freedom in the context of justice, individual expression, and equal chance for success, her service models that of Christ.

Whether teaching lay individuals or health professionals, the messages from nurse leaders on the leading edge of change are worthy of incorporating into one's values. Benner, in her work on the progressive stages of practice and currently in her report of schools of nursing for the Carnegie Foundation, has extended a call for transformation in the education and practice of nurses to meet the demands of society (Benner, Sutphen, & Day, 2009; Benner, in the IOM report "The Future of Nursing: Leading Change, Advancing Health," (2010). This is dependent on a collaborative learning environment and the blending of didactic knowledge, self-knowledge, and maturing affective characteristics. The technology of the internet and personal computerized assistants provide the learner with unlimited exposure to cultural and health-related information to facilitate discovery. Make your computerized tools work for your efficiency, professional growth, and connectivity to those you serve and those who serve alongside you.

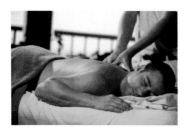  

NOTES . . .

Chapter Three

Define and characterize congregational nursing and its relationship to community health

OBJECTIVES

1. What is it like to be a congregational nurse? The role of congregational nurse is described by day and week, emphasizing the expanse of influence in community.

2. What brings you here? Through Biblical examples a "call" to the profession and the specialty is described.

3. How may the nurse be a spiritual agent?

4. How does congregational nursing fit into the picture of the present health care crisis?

What Does a Parish/Congregational Nurse Do?

Nurses who work in non-acute settings in the community are different from the hospital nurse who manages patient's technical treatments and personal care needs, interprets the doctor's explanations, and monitors the patient's response to medications and treatments. The community nurse has an understanding of the physical forces of the body as it reacts with exposure to disease and injury, but here attention is given to the bigger picture of the home and the other people in the life of the patient, the spiritual condition, as well as the resources in the community that can assist that person in obtaining a quality of life.

So, as I describe the typical activities of a registered, professional Congregational Nurse, think about his/her role not as a "hands-on" nurse you have seen working in the hospital, but as:

A Teacher/Educator:

•Explaining the process of one's disease or condition and reasons for treatment. Then informing about wholistic ways to aid in the treatment and showing how to prevent those problems again.

•Teaching about ways to manage one's health in a wellness mode (Might be done through health fairs, audio-visual presentations, group discussions, poster show, etc.)

•Teaching how to negotiate assistance from other community sources

•Demonstrating infant care to a new mother

•Showing how to become a better parent

•Teaching volunteers how to assist people in need

A Coordinator of Care:

•Identifying physical, mental, emotional, social, or spiritual needs and assisting individuals in finding resources for help. Many of these needs can be met right in the faith community through social support.

A Counselor:

•Responding to times of transition: birth, marriage, divorce, bereavement and grief, change of jobs, children leaving home, etc. Offering a listening ear, assessing for further support, praying, helping individuals obtain spiritual strength and community resources.

•Assisting the clergy in visitation, program planning

<u>An Advocate</u>

•Helping individuals to realize empowerment to make their needs known and to seek their own resources. Bringing appropriate services to dis-enfranchised people. Speaking out for their needs if necessary. Helping to assure their right to a quality of life.

Through all of these roles the Parish (or Congregational) Nurse complements health activities in other sections of the community by fostering partnerships, promoting healthy ways of living across the lifespan, disease prevention strategies, and gaining mental/emotional/spiritual strength through faith. The difference may be that spirituality is woven into all that is done with the goal of bringing members closer to God, the true Source of their life's power.

Their role in finding members who desire to aid others and training them for special ministries brings about an extension of health care from institutions into the community as a health ministry--a new partner in prevention and wholistic health care. The church is recognized as the most effective place in the community to promote health to. *See the Operations Manual **Appendices** for Can and Cannot Do Handout.*

A <u>Week</u> in the Life of a Congregational/Parish Nurse

The amount of time the church-based nurse devotes to the needs of the faith community is determined by the formal contract established between the nurse and the congregation leaders. It may be a paid position for full-time or part-time, it may a stipend position, or it may be a voluntary position in which space, telephone, and other church resources are pledged to support the function of the nurse. It is likely that in the latter situation, the nurse will have other full- or part-time employment so that the hours are limited for the church responsibility.

However, we may presume that the following activities might take place over a week's time.

•A meeting with clergy and/or staff to share information about members in need and to coordinate visitation and to enhance personal, interpersonal, and corporate relationships in the context of spirituality. Also discussing various programs and activities the nurse is engaged in and collaborating with,

•Assessing needs of members both informally and formally; seeking out the dis-enfranchised, the isolated, the grieving and those wanting to be involved,

•Planning programs to meet those expressed and observed needs: may be for age groups, for those needing or those giving care, may be ethnic groups,

•Attending member ministry or support groups to guide or counsel in health-related ways,

•Identifying volunteers who want to serve; conducting volunteer training sessions; coordinating them with people in need,

•Planning and implementing health screening events that are regularly scheduled, perhaps recruiting other health professionals to participate, (Blood pressure screening after the service is one typical event.)

•Responding to calls for advice, counsel, a visit to the home,

•Hospital and extended care visitation,

•Conducting a parenting class, a nutrition seminar, or other health education,

•Leading a health council,

•Participating in planning a community event such as a health fair, a walk-a-thon, etc.,

•Keeping in touch with other community health activities; serving on health-related committees; joining other health professionals to advocate for services such as transportation,

•All the while keeping careful documentation of activities for reporting effectiveness of your practice, justifying your practice, maintaining your case records. The Miller & Carson article (2010) is an excellent resource.

A <u>Day</u> in the Life of a Congregational/Parish Nurse

Because this nurse works *among* city faith communities (churches) and serves individuals *unconnected* to those churches, much of the energy and time will be spent in casefinding and creating resource links for people who may be living marginally in the community. It is a mission outreach. The nurse may serve more than one congregation.

Let us imagine a typical day for the Urban Congregational/Parish Nurse . . .

•The day may begin with a staff meeting and prayer service with a particular faith community (with pre-determined rotation schedule set in collaboration with each sponsoring church).

•Next, home visits based on priority/urgency of need may be made in the city. During that visit, a wholistic assessment would be made, teaching based on observed or expressed need, coordination with community organizations or agencies that might be appropriate, and linking with prepared volunteer from either of the sponsoring churches. Inquiry is made into history and preference of faith community. Documentation is done. Case management plans may be put into place. If other nurse-led agencies are involved, then a collaborative relationship is forged.

•Hospital visits for spiritual support may be included in the rounds of visits.

•Time on the phone to connect volunteers with people in need and to coordinate care through community services. Responding to incoming calls from clients, answer messages, make appointments.

•A lunch committee meeting with other community nurses to consult about clients' needs an existence or lack of services, plan events together for the community.

•More visits or planning or conducting a health promotion event

•Paperwork: record-keeping, reporting, etc. (Refer to Miller & Carson article, 2010)

A Full Day.

What Brings You Here?

Now that light has been shed on the role of the congregational nurse, you probably seek a better understanding of the functions that would make it different from nursing practice outside the body of faith. To the Christian nurse there may be little difference in one's demeanor, attitudes, and critical thinking; and that may be because the nurse has responded to a "call" to enter the profession, whether the arena of practice is in acute care, schools, helicopters, mission field, or congregation.

While there is no established pattern for the manner through which an individual arrives at a decision to take a certain direction in life, in retrospect one sees how the puzzle pieces of circumstances fell into place. Often in the realm of public humanitarian service the attraction is characterized as a "calling" through a long-held dream or an episodic vision. A model adult who exemplifies the perceived ideal in a profession or vocation may influence a career choice; or an experience in the context of extreme human need may elicit a strong response in one's inner being to intervene with skills and knowledge to improve the same or similar witnessed circumstances.

Using Biblical examples which changed nations and even the world, Saul of Tarsus comes to mind. He knew he was doing God's bidding in capturing, imprisoning, and witnessing for conviction many newly converted Christian Jews who were later executed. Then, that blinding Presence which brought him around to the reality interrupted his mission. In Christ's just kingdom persecution is lawlessness. As a result of mentoring by a God-sent humble man and personal soul-searching and prayer, he became a catalyst of Christian hope whose teachings would revolutionize societies of the future. (Acts, Ch. 9)

Moses of Biblical Old Testament times—1500s BC in fact—was called by God for a purpose: to rescue His chosen people out of Egyptian bondage to a land of promise. So when the LORD saw that he turned aside to look, God called to him from the midst of the bush and said, "Moses, Moses!" And he said, "Here I am." (Exodus 3:4) While the "call" was dramatic—an unearthly voice from an uncanny burning desert scrub—the conversation was engaging, to say the least. Moses had become so humbled after 40 years in an agricultural occupation that he begged off from God's assignment. Though he had been taught by a Godly Jewish biological mother about his destiny to be a leader of his enslaved people, he was raised in Pharaoh's house to be an educated, princely government leader. You may read about the circumstances which brought him to the desert and 40 years later to the bush in Exodus Ch. 1-4.

There are many incidences of dramatic alterations in public and private lives in the Bible; it is an historical account of civilization where God reveals His power and purposes to mankind through traceable events and influences. Paul, the previously notorious Saul of Tarsus, instructs us that it is the Holy Spirit of God who hovers over us and moves our conscience to listen to God's inaudible invitation to a life change (Romans 8:9-14; I Corinthians 2:9-13; I Corinthians 3:16). He also teaches that the Holy Spirit orchestrates or coordinates the development and use of normal attributes (not paranormal abilities) or "gifts" in us "for the common good" of society (I Corinthians 12:1-11). One of those is *discernment*; the use of this gift reveals to our "heart" what the logic of the thinking mind directs. We then understand the "call."

So, whether you were called to the nursing profession or not, you apparently sense a calling to minister in a faith environment in the context of a spiritual witness. Everything you know about nursing practice is needed in this role. However, you have opportunity to spend the time you wish to invest in applying the skills of listening and guiding. The integration of spiritual mediation in the act of nursing employs the caring mechanisms and the concepts of therapeutic communication, motivational interviewing, and facilitation of commitment. You will complement the care your colleagues give in other locations and open doors for collaboration for the sake of the whole community.

The Nurse is a Spiritual Agent

A nurse who recognizes the call of God to serve individuals through the means of health promotion and the application of nursing science is a spiritual agent. Christ's ministry is demonstrated through critical thinking applied to care planning, through the comforting touch, and through the skillful methods used to facilitate healing. Like Moses, the nurse must maintain communication with the **PowerSource**. How is that done?

If one has invited the Holy Spirit into the life, leading toward a potential relationship with others, then the environment of the relationship one has with another (the patient's room, a front porch, the car, the airplane, the elevator, etc.) is pregnant with blessing and is "holy ground."

In the history of nursing, the spiritual posture of nurses was dependent on their educational background. The nursing schools of the early 20th century were usually within a faith-based institution – hospitals for the most part. Nursing was a "calling" with a moral intent. A nurse had an occupation, a mission. Nursing was considered an art of comforting patients who were under the care of the physician.

By the 50s and 60s, after nurses proved their intelligent worth during World War II, nursing took on professional characteristics and progressed to a science participating in research. Nursing schools were becoming situated in colleges and universities. Discussion centered around autonomy of practice and practice standards and accountability. Less was said about the spiritual essence of nursing.

By the 70s and 80s the profession was recognized for holistic care and environmental skills of psychosocial dimensions with a reawakening of interest in all spheres of the whole person. It was conceptualized as a balance of art and science. Health care regulations were driving models of practice.

In the mid-90s Jean Watson boldly stated, "At its most basic level nursing is a human-caring, relational profession. It exists by virtue of an ethical-moral ideal, and commitment to provide care for others." What is the spiritual posture in the 21st century, a post-modern world? With a mix of generations and a mix of cultures in the workplace settings, nurses experience varying goals and differing attitudes toward care and caring. What are your spiritual gifts? (See **Spiritual Gifts Module** in the Appendices)

Nurses as spiritual agents bring comfort, solace, and hope to their patients in their pain and distress. Today's care setting has interrupted the milieu in ways that make the performance of this calling difficult. In order to skillfully prepare for the moments of opportunity to do so, knowing how to arrive at "holy ground" and how to conduct a "holy conversation" is necessary. Natural remedies are within the practice guidelines of nursing and can serve as adjuncts to the spiritual intervention. Framing these approaches to practice is a practice ethic. Working collaboratively and harmoniously with colleagues of various generations and ethnicity enhances the intent to bring healing through a wholistic environment.

Critical Need and the Nursing Crisis

As I mentioned in the Preface, extensive efforts are being made to address what we presently see and what is to come in the shortfall of health professionals to care for the nation's health care needs, and especially nurses. In the 2010 Future of Nursing report from the IOM nurses individually and collaboratively in their organizations are urged to develop appropriate leadership competencies. In that Peter Buerhaus (2011) states, "In fact, the report suggests that neither the profession nor patient care can advance through the complexities of contemporary change and transformation without developing a renewed focus on leadership capacities at every level of practice."   I interpret that to mean congregational nursing as well.

In the following excerpt from the IOM you will see the importance placed upon efforts to increase nursing workforce capacity, particularly so in our communities where health promotion and prevention education can reduce health care cost and the burden upon health care professionals, families, and societies.

"In 2009 the *Initiative on the Future of Nursing,* a collaborative effort between the Robert Wood Johnson Foundation (RWJF) and the Institute of Medicine (IOM), undertook a major study on the future of nursing during a critical period in the history of the U.S. health care system. The health care reform debate in Congress and throughout the nation revealed many questions and unknowns. Yet one theme to emerge was the necessary re-examination and re-imagination of the role of nurses to take on challenges facing the profession and to help fulfill the promise of a reformed health care system—improving health. . .
Many important messages emerged from the forum, including:
• Budgets for public health and community health programs are being cut at a time when these programs are needed most to care for aging populations and when greater emphasis is being placed on prevention, wellness, chronic disease management, and moving care into the community.
• Nursing in the community occurs through partnerships with many other individuals and organizations, and nurses need to take a leadership role in establishing these vital partnerships.
Fostering this type of collaboration could improve the continuum of care between acute and community care settings.
• Technology has the potential to transform the lives of nurses providing care in the community, as well as their patients, just as it is transforming commerce, education, communications, and entertainment for the public.
• Varying scopes of practice across states have, in some cases, prevented nurses from providing care to the fullest extent possible at the community level.
• Nurse-managed health clinics offer opportunities to expand access; provide quality, evidence-based care; and improve outcomes for individuals who may not otherwise receive needed care. These clinics also provide the necessary support to engage individuals in wellness and prevention activities.
• Nursing students need to have greater exposure to principles of community care, leadership, and care provision through changes in nursing school curricula and increased opportunities to gain experience in community care settings.
• The delivery of quality nursing care has the potential to provide value across community settings and can be achieved though effective leadership, policy, and accountability."

Practicing nurses and nurse educators have embraced the organizational theory of "transformational leadership," which arose out of a non-nursing discipline as early as 1978. Much has been written about modeling nursing practices after it. The focus of this style of visionary leadership is on effecting change or improvements in an organization through building trust among subordinates and peers, creating unity and creativity with a collective purpose, offering internal rewards of achievement or affirmation and thus motivating toward collaborative and cooperative behavior change or structural alterations. Jackson, Clements, Averill, and Zimbro (2009) question the wisdom of adopting this theory, arguing that individuals who choose nursing as a career are already motivated by internal rewards. They posit that in this time of economic constraint, unpredictable health care, and the nursing shortage, a theory of "holistic, dynamic, inclusive, flexible, and adaptable" characteristics is more appropriate. They have combined the growing quiver of knowing patterns first introduced by Carper in 1978 in terms of empirics, esthetics, personal knowledge, and ethics, with additional patterns of sociopolitical knowing, unknowing, and emancipatory knowing. To the authors, these attributes serve the relational needs of the patient and address the functions of nursing leadership in the wider context of healing through nursing care. Further study of their article (see bibliography) will illustrate how the theory works.

As we consider innovative approaches to delivering nurse services further upstream from acute/tertiary care settings where life is held in the balances under extremely costly circumstances to body, soul, and spirit, congregational nursing offers an attractive and reasonable model. It is a model that should be redesigned to include interventions to all age groups, all races/ethnicities, all socioeconomic levels using technological advances, and collaborating with all other nursing practices in the community.

NOTES . . .

Chapter Four

The Parish Nurse applies the Nursing Process through role and function

In this chapter the role and functions of the Congregational Nurse are examined in the context of relationships to the congregation, the pastor, the community. Through the example of the Connections of Hope Operations Manual an imaginary Congregational Nursing Service is established in Anytown, USA. Examples of the collaborative relationships are discussed here.

A. *Roles of a Congregational Health Nurse*

H - Health Counselor
Here the nurse may augment and reinforce education about treatment initiated in the office of the primary care provider.

E - Educator of Wholistic Health
Health screenings, health seminars, health fairs, websites, newsletters, radio programming may be methods of education.

A - Advocate/Resource Person
Instructing individuals in self-care and decisionmaking and speaking for individuals to health-related service entities; being available for questions and needed health information.

L - Liaison to Community Services
Attending or serving on committees or boards of community organizations where collaboration toward addressing citizen needs may be discussed, leads to further services or development of policies that benefit congregants as well as community at large.

T - Teacher of Volunteers/Groups
Much of what the congregational nurse does is teaching. By preparing volunteers and authorizing and guiding groups the work and influence of the role can be extended and enhanced.

H - Healer: Body, Mind, Spirit
Participating in the refreshing, repairing, and restoring of the whole person confers the attribute of healer.

B. *The Helping Relationship*
What preparation should the nurse of the congregation have to take on the roles mentioned above?

Ideally, the nurse should enter the role as a bachelor's level nurse so that there is an understanding of the particular practice in the community setting and so that the knowledge, skills, and abilities of leadership and management are acquired. Then, of course, the role calls for a life committed to spiritual beliefs and values consonant with the faith body in which you work. Attributes of trustworthiness, dedication, empathy and caring, and love are a must.

Refer to "Congregation as Community" presentation for an overview of the helping relationship, conduct the self-inventory, review the guidelines regarding therapeutic communication.

C. Working with families and groups

What is required to work well in assessing, counseling, guiding, educating, families and groups is the skillful employment of development, social behavior, and communication theories. This is an important component of the toolkit of the congregational nurse and without these skills, effectiveness in all roles will suffer.

D. Building community partnerships with a systems approach

You will notice this topic arises often in this book. Reaching out beyond the walls of the congregation for resources to aid those you serve is a necessity. Connecting with the schools, other churches, the health care system, civic groups, voluntary organizations, recreational organizations, the media, industry is a privilege. Those relationships will not only strengthen your services but they will enlarge the influence and witness of the faith body and create bonds that bring spiritual prosperity to your community at large.

E. The function: What do people usually come to the congregational nurse for?

The problems are no different than those the nurse encounters in any nursing practice environment: anxiety, emotional problems, loss of health or body function, imminent death, relationship crises, unexplained signs and symptoms, etc. The nurse responds according to the level of clinical preparation. In addition, it is important to early clarify with the congregation and the leadership exactly what the nurse's role is in the congregation and to assure them that partnerships and liaisons established with the community are acceptable and of benefit. [Refer to **Stories and Scenarios** in Appendices for examples.]

F. Leadership opportunities and strategies

Refer to the role of Coordinator, connecting caring service and resources with congregants in need in Operations Manual.

G. Requirements and Scope and Standards of Practice

Faith Community Nursing "focuses on the intentional care of the spirit as part of the process of promoting wholistic health and preventing or minimizing illness in a faith community." Refer to and purchase a copy of *The Scope and Standards of Faith Community Nursing* published by the collaborative efforts of the American Nursing Association and Health Ministries Association in 2005. Also refer to the Operations Manual.

H. Particular qualifications, skills and acumen

Refer to both Chapter 6 and the Operations Manual for a job description.

I. Ethical concerns.

As with any nursing role, professional liability insurance coverage is a must. With regard to services to the congregants, typical concerns that may arise about which the nurse will form accountability are: (1) allocation of scarce resources to provide services, (2) truth-telling, (3) life/death concerns, (4) consent for confidential services, (5) development and authentication of the role of congregational nurse, (6) human resource management.

J. Recruiting and Managing Volunteers

The Operations Manual describes in detail how the volunteer serves Connections of Hope and example processes for recruiting, training, and managing a volunteer corps, without which, congregational health services would falter.

K. Congregational Health models

In Chapter One of the Operations Manual eight practice model designs are outlined:

1. Paid Model

2. Volunteer Model

3. Hospital/Agency Paid Model

4. Hospital/Agency Volunteer Model

5. Congregational Consortium Paid Model

6. Faith-based Primary Care Model

In the primary care model the activities of congregational nursing, which include health promotion, health screening, physical and emotional support programs, counseling, and health teaching, further include primary care and case management in communities with high risk, economically deprived, and vulnerable populations. Given the future projections of health care demand weighed against the proportionally declining numbers of nurses and physicians, this model in the church may bring a partial solution to access to health care. Refer to the Trofino, et, al. (2000) article for more information.

Nurses are Needed in Communities of Faith!

NOTES . . .

Chapter Five

GOAL:
Care Management: Define and characterize it; Explain how it can be integrated in a congregational nursing program in a world of health care reform and scarce resources

A. Comparing Home Health Nursing with Congregational Nursing

Home Health Nursing is a practice that is firmly rooted in the community, with a focus on the individual in the home setting, either isolated or surrounded by family and/or neighbors and friends. Services of nursing, companion, housekeeping, or therapies are provided to promote, maintain, or restore health in order to maximize the level of independence one can attain or, at the least, assure quality of life. Because the services are prescriptive, the primary care provider (PCP) issues orders to the agency for services billable to the patient's insurance company. Managing care for the chronically ill or disabled in the home avoids the need for hospital admission or a move to a long-term care facility, both being more costly. Post-operative recovery is accelerated in the home setting also. Home health care then is a form of case management in that the nurse, under the PCP's orders, performs treatments, monitors medications and their effects, assesses patient and environment, instructs and educates in self-care or decisionmaking, coaches toward rehabilitation, and promotes health of the patient and the in-home caregiver and, possibly, the family. All of these activities are founded on knowledge of social, behavioral, teaching/learning, and physical science theories. Because it takes place in the community, social and other health-related conditions of the home and the neighborhood are noted and other resources can be coordinated to serve the patient's needs.

Depending on the pre-determined level of engagement the nurse and/or the congregation leader(s) set, the congregational nurse may mirror some of these services. If he/she is an advance practice nurse and a PCP, opportunities for augmenting overburdened home health care services in the community at large may greatly improve access to health care for the congregation and others.

B. Define and describe the functions of case managers involved in direct care

The functions of the home health nurse embody Case Management (CM). There are many rich and comprehensive definitions of the term; probably the best is that of the Case Management Society of America itself: "a collaborative process of assessment, planning facilitation and advocacy for options and services to meet an individual's health needs through communication and available resources to promote quality cost-effective outcomes." CM is charged with effecting coordination of care that minimizes confusion, eliminates duplication of services, assures continuity of care, minimizes development of further health problems, promotes independence, and reduces overall costs. CM nurses typically function as advance practitioners prepared at least at the BSN level and certified. They may perform in a generalist or a specialist model, their services may be episodic (acute care) or longitudinal (home health or mental health), and they may have minimal tasks, they may only coordinate services and people, or they may provide comprehensive services. The CM role may include some or all of these: (1) clinical expert, (2) consultant, (3) manager of care (4), educator, (5) negotiator/broker, (6) advocate, (7) change agent, (8) counselor, (9) ethicist.

C. Integrate the conceptual model of CM into congregational nursing.

When one reviews the *Scope and Standards of Practice for Faith Community Nursing*, it becomes obvious that this specialty is predicated at one level on managing care of individuals or population groups as a Case Manager would. Practice begins with the Nursing Process components with 4 sub-functions augmenting Implementation of the Plan of Care: Coordinator, Health Teaching & Promoting, Consultation, and Prescriptive Authority (where it applies). After Evaluation, the latter 9 standards refer to the integrity of performance (nursebooks.org). Some examples of integration might be:

1. <u>End-of-life care.</u> Preparing and educating caregivers in personal care factors of comfort and nutrition; Recruiting volunteers to be sitters who offer to read, play instruments, sing, massage, write letters, etc. Monitor comfort level, meds, hygiene, intake and elimination. Coordinate with PCP.

2. <u>Disabled child with vent.</u> Collaborating with PCP and other nurses or therapists. Arranging respite care for the parents/caregivers from among congregants. Home spiritual education to the child. If attends school, seek ways volunteers may assist.

3. <u>Returning soldier, with functional deficits d/t injury.</u> Collaborate with the VA in providing continuity of care for rehabilitation. Observe for untoward signs of behavioral or mental changes. Facilitate acceptance and enculturation into the faith community. Wholistically assess family for needs. Arrange transportation services.

Case Studies: *Application of the Nursing Process with the addition of "Monitoring" and "Care Coordination"*

In the Appendices there are 6 case studies of soon-to-be-discharged adults who will need home health nursing services. Select one and imagine they are returning to your faith community. You, as congregational nurse will be involved in supplementing care. Liven the case with what you know about your environment and create a care map depicting the individuals (volunteers) you will recruit and the tasks they will be instructed to perform, determine activity needs, transportation needs, nutrition needs, spiritual needs, etc.

A text entitled *Clinical Case Studies in Home Health Care* (2011), edited by Leslie Neal-Boylan and published by Wiley Blackwell would be an excellent resource about typical cases of conditions affecting all body systems managed by community nurses.

Chapter Six

Developing a heart for spiritual leadership

If you have come to the crossroads of decision on whether or not to become a congregational nurse for your faith community (or of another faith community), you may be experiencing some anxiety over your readiness for the role or over feelings of inadequacy that you never felt in other clinical practice settings. First of all, you will be working autonomously, sometimes making independent decisions that may forever impact on the quality of life of those you serve. You will not have close oversight and administrative resources a nurse in most health care facilities has. You will be responsible for your continuing education and professional linkages. You will be taking initiative on many fronts. What an opportunity!

Perhaps you are concerned about your spiritual preparation for the role. Do you have the requisite "gifts" to minister in a variety of ways? Will your life and lifestyle model wellness? Will you know what to say/do for anxious or grieving people? In this chapter, there are resources to inspire your own self-study into Scripture.

You may look into your own spiritual well-being by assessing 3 basic factors: (1) the dimension of your faith in God and of your belief in the scope of His power, (2) the degree to which you feel control over your daily life and the relative proportion God has control of, (3) and the dimension of satisfaction you have with your life and who you are. As you develop your spiritual connection with the Source of power you will find it more comfortable to initiate and maintain discussion in this dimension with those you serve. You will have the power to be intentional about entering "holy ground" with them and speaking of spiritual concerns. Remember the experience Moses had at the burning bush? (Chapter One). You can have that too. Let's continue to discuss this.

A. Spiritual Gifts
A learning module of Spiritual Gifts with Biblical texts is provided in the Appendices. Use this to determine what your gifts are and how they will serve your role as congregational nurse. The United Methodist Church provides an interesting teaching video of the spiritual gifts from a diverse perspective. Watch it at http://www.umc.org/site/c.lwL4KnN1LtH/b.1355371/k.9501/Spiritual_Gifts.htm

Other inventories you may take online are found at:

http://www.kodachrome.org/spiritgift/

http://www.churchgrowth.org/cgi-cg/gifts.cgi?intro=1

B. Spiritual distress defined
Spiritual distress can be defined as an experience of profound disharmony in the patient's/client's belief or value system that threatens the meaning of the client's life. The meaning of life is questioned. Once spiritual assistance is sought, the individual voices guilt, or loss of hope, or spiritual emptiness, or a feeling of being alone. He/She appears anxious, depressed, discouraged, fearful, or angry. Some related factors may be separation: from loved ones, from religious ties. He may be experiencing a chronic or

debilitating illness, surgery, pain, of loss of loved one. You are in a position to bring refreshment and restoration to his soul.

C. Christian counseling principles

Some characteristics highly desirable in a congregational nurse can be found in the Operations Manual:

- Have a relationship with God

- Possess an empathetic personality along with well-developed diplomatic skills and a senses of responsibility and confidentiality

- Be psychologically and spiritually mature with a special desire and aptitude for pastoral ministry

- Practice nursing using wholistic health care principles

Educational and experiential preparation for the nursing profession rests on what used to be called "therapeutic communication". Essentially, that means the application of ethical principles concerning preserving the integrity of the individual served through fairness, truthfulness, confidentiality, self-determination, and benevolence (kindness), enabling a free flow of discussion that may be directed into productive and solution-based actions. The expected outcome is that the individual with his/her family, friends, and others will enjoy peace and purpose.

The nurse in the faith community needs a reliable spiritual assessment tool with which to direct the discussion and to uncover unspoken concerns of the individual served. It should be broad enough in scope to address the variance of spirituality in personalities, the depth of meaningful relationships which may be significant in healing, the perceptions of ties, obvious signs of distress, an inventory into one's inner resources to cope with difficulty, a family genogram, and finally an assessment of one's personal belief system and personal faith practices. I offer in the Appendices of the Operations Manual a **Spiritual Assessment** to fit the requirements. It is a collection of the best and most appropriate to nursing in the congregation that I could obtain from various faith-based organizations and chaplains.

D. The Continuum of Care

As mentioned above, the congregational nurse is an important link in the chain of health care delivery because the role guides many functions that reach people along the span of life and the continuum of health to illness and death. It is a privileged place to be---somewhere between the first breath of life, through various stations of the lives of people, in the wonder of healing, at the last moment of life. The focus is on facilitating healing as opposed to curing, to connecting to resources rather than only hands-on care, to comforting, and to being present without interruption.

Chapter Seven

GOAL:
Building collaborative relationships with clergy and congregation

For over 2,000 years the Biblically-founded Christian church has been at the center of the lives of believers, serving as a fountain of faith, hope, and connections with the family of faith and the God they worshipped. From earliest times it has acted to restore God's image in men, women and children through lifestyle, traditions, anecdotes, witness of God's work in the life, and healing ministrations. These attributes were not confined to members of the faith, but extended to the community at large and abroad to other or foreign countries. Before there were physicians or nurses there were practicing healers who depended on God to effect restoration of health or comfort in death. A loving congregation of faith must practice love to even the unlovely.

Today, clergy, pastors, and chaplains lead believers spiritually and administer programs that aid in carrying out the mission of the church. It is these leaders the congregational nurse must recruit into the acceptance of the nurse as necessary in every congregation, whether dedicated to one or sharing expertise with many. We will spend a little time on the subject of gaining an amicable and beneficial partnership with them. The Operations Manual will also be your guide.

A. How to introduce a nurse-led health ministry to the clergy and the congregation
Because there is benefit in numbers when introducing change, your first step should be to identify all active or recently retired health professionals in your congregation, with particular notice of nurses. Gain their support for a health ministry and their solidarity with you in approaching the clergy or pastor with a well-considered plan. Here you may encounter some resistance, for various reasons: ignorance about the role of a congregational nurse, fear of loss of control over leadership, cost, fear of liability issues for example. If there is resistance some time will be needed to educate the leadership and to prepare a proposal to submit to the Board, or even the district conference office if necessary.

In the process of these negotiations it is important to know how to make your intentions known and accepted by informal leaders of the congregation in quiet, unobtrusive meetings with one or a few at a time to explain what you believe to be an important ministry and why. If you are not familiar with group dynamics, persuasion strategies, and opinion-setting in your favor, do some research into the topic or consult with the premier supporting organization for faith community nursing—International Parish Nursing Resource Center at http://www.parishnurses.org/ .

B. Organizing the program - Getting started
Once you have the authorization from the leadership and a strategic plan is formed, you will educate the congregants about your role and function through visual aids, newsletters, presentations, social networking, and whatever means appropriate. You may wish to begin your services with a health screening event or a nutrition/cooking class followed by a picnic. Begin visiting those you identify as in need of a nurse. At the earliest convenience a health assessment is conducted of the faith community so that programs and services can be planned and individuals and families have opportunity to express what they would like to enjoy from the ministry. From the beginning there must be a mechanism that informs everyone continually that there is a nurse in the congregation.

Now that you are on a roll, you will probably need a health council or cabinet to aid and advise you and, perhaps, a volunteer coordinator. The first task the council should assume is to help you set a budget and secure reliable financial support, whether as a paid staff member or as a volunteer. You will need documentation on insurance against liability. Writing an operations manual with policy, procedures, job descriptions, and documentation forms for programs and services is also an early priority. Developing interventions and procedures and setting policies for services are a necessity to assure accountability in practice. A computer software program to aid in documentation is a must.

You and the volunteers (hopefully nurses among them) will build a library and media center for health promotion and education purposes and for consulting on practice issues. A computer dedicated to the ministry and password protected should be housed in your office behind a lockable door. Equipment and project or program materials should be dedicated to this purpose and stored in a lockable closet. As you peruse the Operations Manual other suggestions may be helpful in getting your congregational nursing practice started.

Continue on to the next chapter to read how to organize volunteers to assist you and congregants in the programs and services you wish to establish.

Chapter Eight

GOAL:
Building a force of volunteers to extend, enhance, and enable nursing services in the faith community

The experienced nurse will recognize that a reliable force of volunteers possessing the same purpose and whose beliefs and behaviors are consistent with the values and beliefs of the congregation are priceless in facilitating a program of helping services. The number and age of volunteers will depend on the size of congregation, and maybe more than that, on the number and complexity of services you wish to provide. When you are planning for these services your first consideration for volunteer activities should be the structure and environment in which they will work. Their leadership and management and the conditions under which they work should mirror a beneficial environment as much as possible, even more so because they are not getting reimbursed for their time and effort in helping. Here are some tips:

1. Create an atmosphere which values volunteers, both as individuals and for the work they do.

   • Treat volunteers as you would an honored guest.

   • Greet volunteers individually when they arrive for a training or service.

   • Provide many opportunities for volunteers to contribute their own experience/expertise; and honor all points of view.

   • Monitor volunteers' physical and emotional well being throughout training and tenure.

   • Create as attractive, hygienic, and safe a physical environment as possible.

   • Thank volunteers frequently for their participation.

   2. Create community and build personal connections—among volunteers and between volunteers and their manager.

   • Provide them with training guidelines to establish mutual respect.

   •Plan periodic social events to honor them and facilitate friendship-building.

   • Organize their assignments in varying small groups to widen friendship ties and build teamwork ideals

3. Create opportunities for personal exploration, expression, and growth.

   • Use activities that provide opportunities for volunteers to explore and express their own values. Introduce them to a spiritual gifts inventory.

   • Use case studies as opportunities for volunteers to explore what clients' lives are like and how to handle difficult situations with a client.

   • Use small groups as opportunities for quieter people to express themselves.

   • Create activities that allow for exploration of people's feelings about loss and other emotional experiences associated with volunteer work.

   • Use real plays rather than role-plays to practice skills. In real plays, people speak about issues that are real and current in their lives rather than playing a role.

- Focus discussions on how people bring who they are as a person to the volunteer work they do.

- Use opening/closing prayer circles at the beginning/end of each meeting together.

4. Create opportunities to explore the nature and rewards of service.

- Have volunteers work on a client case study in small groups to identify the ways they could   be of service to a client.

- Use real plays in counseling skills practice, giving the listener an experience of the rewards of serving another by listening, and the speaker an experience of the rewards of being served.

- Have a panel of clients and/or experienced volunteers talk about their relationships and the rewards of being of service.

5. Provide necessary information, skills, and skills practice.

- Use case scenarios to illustrate the purpose of their work.

- Discuss what works well in participants' experience in small groups, then report results to the whole group.

- Use technology in training sessions as well as printed matter (videos, internet sites)

- Dedicate a room for simulation training of various volunteer activities they will engage in.

A. How to mobilize and prepare volunteers to assist: Promoting followers
If the nurse is new to the congregation, learning about skilled volunteers or interested individuals willing to be trained will come by recommendations. A good **Recommendation Form** should provide a convincing profile of observed performance, attitude, and dependability. There is an example on Page 19 in the Operations Manual. Educational and awareness-building presentations to the congregation should always include an appeal for volunteers for specific needs. Include teens as much as possible so that they may understand the duty of service and realize the blessing of helping.

B. Training and maintaining the volunteer force
In the Operations Manual you will find guidelines for managing volunteers and their services as well as supporting documents for recruitment. The volunteer who is acutely observant and mindful of matching expressed or unexpressed need with resources or services that exist or have the potential of being created is invaluable to a congregational nurse program. Groom and mentor them for just such an attribute. They will aid you in case-finding and coordination tasks.

Chapter Nine

GOAL:
Mentoring Would-be Nurses and Volunteers

You, reader, come to this avenue of service with a willing and dedicated spirit. Perhaps you are a relatively new graduate nurse with previous experience in another field. Or maybe you have worked in clinical nursing as a certified expert in cardiac care or orthopedics. A recent certification course in gerontology nursing has sent you in this direction. Or you have led a home health agency as director for 20 years. In whatever capacity, you can probably reflect on a time when you as a nurse in a new leadership position shared a relationship of mutual understanding with a nurse experienced in your position. You were grateful for the personal support she offered to further your professional development. It was a nurturing relationship, perhaps one that will last a lifetime. Then again, as a leader in your specialty, you may have been a mentor to someone else, a newly-prepared manager, perhaps. Mentor, yes; the term is *mentor.* Where did that come from? . . . a little history lesson.

Mentor is a figure out of Greek mythology and the days of Homer and the siege of the city of Troy. When Kind Odysseus left home to engage in the war, he appointed his good friend Mentor in charge of his household and the nurturing of his son, Telemachus. Mentor protected him and guided him into his place in Greek society over the next 10 years. The term was picked up hundreds of years later in French literature and became a way of life across generations, and over time has found it place of influence in leadership and business world language today.

A. *Define Mentoring and describe the mentoring relationship*
Historically, the mentor was superior in knowledge, skill, or experience to the one mentored and the relationship was of a top-down nature, so that the *mentee* became obligated and replicated the skill and intent of the mentor, as in an apprenticeship. One's self-determination was inhibited.

In contrast, Snyder (1995) introduced the concept of *becoming* in a learning relationship in which the counselor, or mentor, operationalized empathy and intimacy into a process where the helping individual tends to "perceive the thoughts, meaning, feelings of the other as somehow also part of the 'self,'" and both then tend to experience a space between and around them of mutual understanding. Nurses strive to reach a place of similar dimension when they give of themselves to the patient-nurse relationship in the context of *presencing* (Fingeld-Connett, 2008). *"Being there"* at the bedside of one dying and offering comfort is an example.

In the mentoring relationship both parties learn, grow, and develop in such a way that both are stimulating each other in their respective roles through intense and emotionally charged responses. There may be an element of risk, calling for established trust and veracity. Both strengths and weaknesses must be openly shared with respect to the learning task at hand. The importance of mentoring relationships grows as society changes, young people emerge from troubled home life, immigrants arrive in a strange environment, adults change careers to assure a needed income, soldiers return from chaotic war zones, and advances in health care require leaders. At each transition in life and each challenge, we need mentors who have an interest in our development, achievement, and success.
So, here are a few chosen definitions of the term Mentor:

- A lifelong relationship in which a mentor helps a protege reach her or his God-given potential. One with someone you like, enjoy, believe in. One in which, over time, you both may reach common ground in development. (Biehl, 1996, p. 19-22).

- What it is not: evangelism or discipleship, apprenticeship, modeling, or based on matching (Biehl, 1996, p. 28)

- An individual with a strong moral and ethical fiber that encourages the mentee to think critically and act skillfully in challenging situations (Marquis & Huston, 2006, p. 390)

B. The Several Roles of the Mentor

- *Example:* Demonstrating expertise and promoting role socialization; role modeling a vision, providing a mirror in which to imagine oneself.
- *Sponsor:* Creating opportunities for individual achievement; facilitates network-building.
- *Coach:* Providing cues about performance, instructing how to improve.
- *Role Model:* The mentee respects the mentor's accomplishments and identifies with the example, evaluating the behaviors and selecting those to emulate—an expression of mutual positive regard. The mentor sets high standards, challenging thought.
- *Counselor:* A psychosocial function the allows the mentee to express concerns, raise issues, seek opinion; and, because the mentor is respected, accepts guidance in confidentiality and may act on it or reject it with the relationship remaining intact.
- *Enculturation teacher:* Lessons are demonstrated and taught of the traditions, practices, mindset, expectations of the environment in which they both work. Broadens perspective and suggests new ways to view situations.

A home healthcare nurse suggested this acronym (Sitzman, 1998, p. 20):

Mindful attention—Give thoughtful and sympathetic professional attention to the nurses around us.

Encouragement—Give positive encouragement to those with whom we work—particularly those who are struggling professionally.

Nurture professional growth—attend professional inservices and continuing education offerings together. Focus on the positive aspects of the experience, even if it's just that you are sharing the experience.

Teach with joy—We all have experiences to share and knowledge to give to others.

Observe and orient as needed—compassionately observe other nurses (especially those new to the profession) and help reorient them in areas where they are struggling.

Recognize and respect the accomplishments and efforts of your co-worker nurses from rookies to seasoned veterans.

C. Characteristics of effective mentors; anyone can; who should?
Key character traits required of a successful and compassionate mentor are: Courtesy, Respect, and Grace. Six necessary components of the role and function which, by example, should inspire others to assume the role of mentor are:

- Passion—this attribute equals commitment in what we do and demonstrates an intensity, a focus, a drive, and a joy to do the task/function over again and again.

- Purpose—know what you are doing; be aware of what you are investing your life in.
- Plan/Path—and with purpose follows a path to where you want to be.
- Partnerships—the mentoring relationship needs a sense of partnership and synchronicity
- Possibilities—realize there is potential in each role with now unknown results.
- Pass It On—mentor mentors—we need more!

What a tremendous opportunity the congregational nurse has in not only modeling to other nurses and health professionals the caring, dedicated, and capable nurse they desire in a "healer", but being the catalyst of growth and perpetuation of the health ministry through more prepared nurses!

View the "Mentoring" PowerPoint in the Presentations section of this volume.

NOTES . . .

Chapter Ten

GOAL:
Acquire Strategies for promoting and building a Health Promotion initiative

The Congregational Nurse contributes to the vision and the mission of the congregation and the body of faith it represents. In Christian churches that is expressed through the metaphor "Restoring the image of God in man." God, as Creator, designed this world and the creatures in it to share in the blessings of His kingdom, to bring pleasure through intimate friendships. In faith communities corporate worship, prayer, listening to or reading His Word, singing praises to Him, and fellowshipping with His earthly family bring health to the soul. Satan, who once led praise services in Heaven, now because of sin tries to destroy the relationship God has with us, His Creatures, by altering our state of health and orchestrating accidents, violent acts, dysfunctional human relationships, filling our minds with doubt and discontent, and thwarting our efforts to believe and trust God. It is the mission of the congregational nurse to mitigate the consequences of sin through benevolent ministries of spiritually-blessed health promoting interventions. This chapter offers a broad scope of opportunities for programming, referencing what other nurses and organizations are doing.

A. Act on expressed needs, observed needs, and desires of the congregation
Before plans are begun for your program, you will have done an assessment of your congregation's needs (See the Operations Manual). You may have already learned of a needs assessment your community at large has done, perhaps by a public or private health system. And you may have researched the databases listed in Chapter One for local data that points to deficits in health indicators. This information will reveal priorities and opportunities for your health initiatives. Keep in mind that what you plan for your own congregants has an impact on the larger community and that conditions out there might elicit an alarm that compels you to prepare a countering education program.

So you have the need and wish lists of your congregation and its leaders and you have local health-related data and you might then envision future needs (changing demographics in the congregation, influx of immigrants, new babies, a flu epidemic in the nation, you name it). Gather your volunteer nurse(s), the clergy or pastor(s), the health council/cabinet and set priorities and begin to assess what you will need in equipment, partners, locations, to name a few categories.

B. Coordinate education events, screenings, etc. of health care facilities and organizations in the community
As leader you will delegate duties for the planned events well in advance with instructions in writing so that your planned activities may be replicated in the future. Begin a contact list in your computer. You may have the support of local healthcare facilities, such as laboratory personnel for screenings, dietitian for nutrition counseling, physical therapist for BMI testing and exercise education. The more you can do in collaboration with other health organizations, the greater your impact on community health and well-being. The Connections of Hope model in the Operations Manual demonstrates community relations and the benefit your volunteers may contribute to other efforts in the community.

C. Demonstrate the uniqueness of faith-based programming

Your programming will showcase what a community of faith can do in improving the health status of individuals with common or special needs. A wholistic lifestyle in which individuals practice mindful attention to daily practices such as, (1) balanced nutrition and weight control, (2) regular strength-building and heart-healthy exercise, (3) generous intake of clean water rather than sodas or coffee, (4) moderate exposure to sunshine to stimulate mood-enhancing serotonin and bone-building Vitamin D, (5) temperance (balance in) all facets of life, (6) plenty of fresh air breathed in, (7) rest and relaxation that the body requires daily, (8) and trust in God's intervention (NEWSTART).

D. Use acceptable and proven models of design--models that work in other communities and congregations

As you can imagine, planning and implementing a health promotion initiative, even a year in programming, is expensive in time, energy, and money. Look for successful examples other faith communities have conducted, examine articles in nursing research literature, or adapt previous programs/events your congregation has provided and add health benefits to those.

For example: A previous fund-raising benefit for an injured child who needed expensive surgery and prolonged rehabilitation might have been a $50-a plate sit-down dinner and a concert. You might add to that a presentation of pool or bicycle safety by the fire and rescue department of your community and a special Safety Camp for children ages 6-11 at the same time.

Another example: Your congregation goes on a yearly camping and hiking retreat for all ages. This time you take along an expert in wilderness survival techniques who also demonstrates the value of each person preparing their own "go-bag" for 3 days survival away from the home when flood, fire, tornado, hurricane has interrupted normal living and there are no sustaining resources set up yet. Here are some resources for know-how:

http://www.ready.gov/america/getakit/index.html

http://www.survival-gear-guide.com/go-bags.html

http://www.firstaid-supply.com/

http://www.popularmechanics.com/science/4220574

http://campingsurvival.com/hugobagkit.html

Examples Health Promotion Initiatives

Birds, Bees and the Bible

"CDC estimates that there are approximately 19 million new STD infections each year, which cost the U.S. healthcare system $16.4 billion annually and costs individuals even more in terms of acute and long-term health consequences." HIV is a preventable sexually transmitted disease (STD), yet the incidence is high in certain populations in the Western World. In the U.S. (latest data from 2009 statistics) the annual number of new HIV infections has been stable (around 48,000-50,000 cases), but there was a 21% increase for people in the 13-29 yr age range, which was driven by a 34% increase in young men-having-sex-with-men (MSM), and Black/African/American MSMs had increased by 48% since 2006. African/Americans comprise only 14% of the population but accounted for 44% of all new HIV infections, while Hispanics represent approximately 16% of the population and account for 20% of new HIV cases (CDC.gov).

The faith community can provide protection to its youth from exposure to STDs through education about risky behaviors and counseling by way of its congregational nurse and health ministry services. Here is what can be learned from a qualitative study in southern Alabama among single mothers of teens who participated in a focus group. Some of their comments were:

Sex education in the school and the home is not enough.

Even a Personal Life Skills course does not educate regarding negotiation skills.

It is difficult to supervise your children when you work full time and date too.

Not everyone can adequately educate their children about sexuality issues.

Often they do not know what to say.

Our culture (media, entertainment, etc.) talk about sex too much, but do not mention consequences.

Church leaders have been silent too long about sexual issues; religious organizations could help parents with discussion skills. The Bible could be used as a tool to empower parents. How many parents can reference Scripture on these issues?

The mothers agreed that a faith-based program about sexuality, behavior, prevention of disease would be welcome if if were grounded in the teachings of the Bible. They suggested the name be "Birds, Bees, and the Bible." (Cornelius, 2009)

An additional and excellent article on this topic is "Protecting Youth from Early and Abusive Sexual Experiences" (Rew and Bowman, 2008).

Exercise and Mental Illness

Obesity is a significant risk factor for Syndrome X or *metabolic syndrome* in which a group of chronic diseases occur (glucose intolerance or diabetes, hyperlipidemia, hypertension, hyperinsulinism, insulin resistance. A 5% increase in body weight puts one at 200% greater risk for developing this syndrome. Individuals with mental illness are prone to be overweight; therefore, intervention is an important concern and psychiatric nurses are attempting to address this problem. Certainly activity must be increased, but if individuals have cognitive and behavioral abnormalities, interventions must reach them where they are in their mental and emotional processes. Weber (2010), conducted an extensive search of the literature to find validation and models of successful exercise programs for those with schizophrenia. She found good examples of programs to reduce or prevent early signs of depression which would be helpful to a congregational nurse.

Psychoeducational Support Groups

Current economic conditions in the world challenge one's ability to cope with stresses and increases concerns for individuals suffering from chronic illness, expensive medical or surgical treatment, or weakening family relationships. The church is an ideal place to offer psychosocial support while also providing education that enables people in trouble to cope and find solutions to their problems. As we know, many physical and mental health problems are rooted in emotional and spiritual struggles; therefore, the congregational nurse can orchestrate support groups with expert facilitation to prevent or ameliorate the physical or mental problems and reduce health care expense. Hurley and Mohnkern (2004) give detailed guidance.

Family and Faith-based Diabetes Prevention Program for Youth
Adolescent overweight and obesity conditions have the nation concerned, to the point of White House initiatives for children and youth to "Get Moving!" With a federal grant a pilot study was conducted in Chicago's south side directed to 29 African American families (62 subjects) with children aged 9-12 years in the 85th percentile or higher body mass index (BMI) and with a family history of diabetes. Exclusion criteria for children included presence of chronic disease or health condition, inability to perform physical exercise, known psychiatric disorder, inability to comply with a restricted diet. The parents were expected to participate in all activities with the children. Extensive pre- and post-measurements were taken in physical, biochemical, and behavioral domains. Key behaviors targeted with 14 weeks of education and coaching were increasing physical activity, increasing fruit and vegetable intake, decreasing fat and overall caloric intake, and decreasing TV watching and sedentary time. The article is quite detailed about the program, providing a wealth of ideas for health programming or even replication of this study (Burnet, et al, 2011).

Spiritual Needs of Victims of Traumatic Brain Injury (TBI)
An unusual study of 61 victims of TBI assessed relationships among spiritual beliefs, religious practices, congregational support, and health (Johnstone, Yoon, Rupright, & Reid-Arndt, 2008) through use of the MOS-Short Form 36 (did you look that up when in Chapter One?) and another questionnaire on religiousness and spirituality. Little research has been done in the area of religion and health and very little with TBI patients, which is alarming because so many soldiers, both men and women, are returning from exposure to blast injury in the war zones. You may have an individual of this population in your congregation. Do you understand what mechanisms he/she is using to cope? Many of these are reported to rely on their religious and spiritual resources to cope with long-term disabilities. Do you know how to reach them?

A major finding in this study was that "individuals with TBI who experienced a stronger sense of meaning in their life and who reported stronger spiritual values/beliefs were more likely to have better self-perceived physical health" (p. 415). Also, those with greater support from their congregation were more likely to report better mental health, but religious practices did not necessarily improve mental health. "In general, the results suggest that the physical and mental health of individuals with TBI may be related primarily to spiritual experiences and congregational social support, but not to specific religious practices (i.e. prayer, reading religious texts, attending religious services, etc.) (p. 416). It is conjectured that worsening health leads to increasing dependence on prayer.

Using Technology for Older Adult Needs
Hawkins (2010) describes a controlled research project that used a videophone for periodically-scheduled calls applying motivational interviewing techniques to educate older adults in self-managing their diabetes. Congregational nurses can be as adaptive and innovative as home health care nurses in efficiently using technology to provide services. As the Boomer population ages and the succeeding cohort reaches their 50's there is more need to maintain contact and persist in health promotion and chronic disease case management or guidance through use of computerized devices, telephony, or

videography. Enlist the computer and audio/visual technicians in your congregation to help you develop a reach -out plan that aids your ministry.

Radio Broadcasting
Do you have homebound individuals in your congregation? For a small investment your congregation may possibly purchase an FM radio spectrum band for spiritual and health-related broadcasting within a radius of 20 miles of your church. It is fun to create radio programs that inform and uplift. There is very good software that will enable you to do so. Here is a source that will locate vacant frequencies in your location http://www.radio-locator.com/cgi-bin/vacant .

Suggested Wellness Activities to Implement

Information/Education
Participation in parish health fair

Workshops on living wills/durable power of attorney/advance directives

Establish a health library/Design a health education speakers program

Write weekly/monthly advice column for church bulletin/newsletter

Staff an information/advice table or consultation room for after services

C.P.R. training classes

Stress management classes

Hygiene program for pre-schoolers; dental health

Organize an information network

Classes/Workshop about budget management and understanding medical bills & insurance

Sabbath-keeping Seminar

Baby-sitting class/ Nursery Attendant Training

Time Management in Context of Spiritual Living

Support
Organize and facilitate visitation programs for the ill/shut-ins

Prepare support groups for bereaved or unemployed

Connect with local crisis intervention network

Collaborate with existing counseling centers

Develop respite program for caregivers

Support group for caregivers

Plan weekend health retreats – Fitness for Life

Organize telephone ministry

Offer the Congregational Nurse center to dependency intervention meetings (AA, NA, etc.)

Maintain a health equipment closet

Organize, train, and facilitate volunteers ministries (i.e., Stephen or Luke Ministries, etc.)

Connect with community support groups and health and human services agencies

Network with the parish nurse movement

Enrichment programs/workshops for all populations

Gifts of the Spirit Workshop

Caring for Elderly Parents/Sandwich Generation Issues

Prevention

Blood pressure, cancer, diabetes, glaucoma, depression, nutrition, cholesterol etc. screenings

Aerobics classes for various populations

Walking programs for shut-ins and others in various environments

Organized day care for adults and/or children

Organize/participate in blood drives

Marriage enrichment, parenting, life planning seminars

Corporate Wellness

Conclusion

Health literacy is a science to itself in this world of pervasive communication. It is often difficult to get the attention of the individuals you wish to reach: posters are ignored, email or phone tree messages are forgotten, advertisement in the media is usurped by a newer topic of greater excitement or interest. Health messages, unless they resonate with an individual's sense of well-being, seem less important. So prevention communication may take a back seat until illness or accident occur. Well, Maibach and Parrott (1995) wrote a book in which principles of designing health messages remains perennial. It is theory-grounded in Prochaska and DiClemente's Stages of Change or Transformational Theory and Bandura's social cognitive theory literature. One example chapter discusses the decision-making approach to risk reduction messages, another addresses how to reach young audiences, another how to apply persuasion with positive messages rather than fear. You may find it quite useful. In this sound-bite world of communication and attention-getting, you may wish to consult the college or university near you which offers health communication studies for collaboration. Professors are always looking for projects for their students. OK, is that enough to inspire you with ideas for your practice? In the next chapter we will discuss community collaborations.

Chapter Eleven

GOAL:
Understand the Value of Interfaith Collaboration; How to Build Effective Relationships and Partnerships in the Community

"Partnering and collaboration are the hallmark of many successful models implemented by practice and academic healthcare settings worldwide. Strategic partnering, within and beyond institutions, provides opportunities for personal and professional growth, outreach, and collaboration. Within the global nursing community, cross-national partnerships represent a vehicle for extending knowledge sharing, and for using on-site visits, tele- and videoconferencing, electronic mail, and other resources. The World Wide Web has opened doors to distance learning programs that were once a dream, and that now represent reality" (Weinstein, 2004). The author goes on to discuss the importance of cultural knowledge, awareness, and sensitivity, most significantly acquired through a lived experience with people of various cultures but certainly obtainable with acute observation skills. She speaks of nurse-to-nurse collaboration in a partnership that serves a diverse society. She states that "nurses are uniquely positioned to move from 'me' to 'we.'"

The "we" that embodies a collaborative relationship might be reached by this method, introduced in England and shared with U.S. nurses through the American Nurses Association. It is described as *reflective practice* in which one examines the here and now (i.e., the people I work with on an average day, the physical and psychological closeness to them, the typical conversation held and the theme that evolves, the interactions with the people served) with visual board objects and reflects on, or considers, what was working in the relationships, what was not, was there good teamwork, how might the communication be improved, etc. (Ross, Kind, and Firth, 2005). It is somewhat like a storyboard concept and it appeals to both the sense of touch and cognition. The congregational nurse might use this exercise alone and then with those she works with on a regular basis to open discussion of building collaboration toward the common goal of ministry.

Clergy/Pastor-Nurse Relationship

Entering into a religion-health care partnership is both a blessing and a challenge. Any time nurses blend the responsibilities of their profession with non-health entities there are bumps in the road that need to be smoothed out through education from both perspectives. Joint priorities should be determined following establishment of a mutual understanding and agreement of the mission of each and of the blended both. Ultimately, your collaborative objective is to restore health to the congregation, and by extension to each individual, by your separate and joint ministries. Once this has been accomplished, you may desire a "working" relationship with other congregations of your faith in the community or region, or you may consider joining in efforts for the common good by congregations not of your particular faith. Either action should be predicated on joint agreement between you as nurse and the congregation leadership.

Interfaith Relationships

The movement of interfaith collaboration is widespread and has resulted in many stories of community and population-specific health improvements. Simpson and King (1999) write of an example in Appalachia where "God brought all these churches together." They inform the reader in their article how the religious entity forms the life patterns and belief systems of its adherents over generations, and compounding the individual case with several types of religious entities into the collection brings diversity and complexity of immense proportions. Individuals then differ in their perceptions of health and how it is achieved; it may range from optimum feelings of well-being and disease free to burdened with several chronic conditions but "I can get out of bed in the morning so I'm good". With this in mind, the researchers sought through qualitative means to understand (1) What are the health-related activities found in religious worship services and practices that may influence the development of religion-health partnerships in a central Appalachian community? and (2) What are organizational activities within and between religious groups that may influence the development of such? This was a primarily Christian community in eastern Kentucky and southern West Virginia. The authors state, "the organizational activities of interdenominational cooperation, outreach service, associations, an local church governance underlie routes to collaboration within and between religious groups in the study region. Knowledge of the formal, informal, and tacit organizations of religious groups is essential when planning religion-health partnerships." (p. 46). The results of their ethnographic study with the inhabitants supported this statement.

There is a national organization begun under the Robert Wood Johnson Foundation in 1983 called Faith in Action (www.fianationalnetwork.org) Out of that funding has sprung several local caregiving programs in which parish nurses have been involved—Waukesha, WI was one of the earliest ones—www.interfaithwaukesha.org.

Characteristics of Building Interfaith Partnerships

A. Defining the faith community in the context of the community at large. Community demographics indicate spiritual health; church attendance and involvement define spiritual health; outreach expresses fervor

You have assessed your faith community and can gauge its health wholistically and you have noted attendance and who does not have contact with it. You next will want to understand the community at large and how it impacts on the health of your congregation. Knowing the community in which your congregation lives and works (knowing about) involves data gathering and engagement in the civic affairs to the degree that you know what the leadership represent and what voluntary health and human services organizations exist to collaborate with.

B. How to become knowledgeable about other congregations in an ever-widening circle in the community.

Look for opportunities to aid other church-led/sponsored outreach. Examples are:
1. Food Banks
2. Homeless shelters
3. Meal sites
4. Community Centers
5. Low income housing neighborhoods
6. Pregnancy crisis centers
7. Abuse shelters

Find ways to integrate your presence into their activities and dialogue about common concerns; find a venue in which you can work together on events or projects. Is there a risk of "diluting" your mission if you do so? Absolutely not! There is so much need in the world that many people slip out of sight without diligent caregivers in the community.

C. Broadening your scope of policy and legislation knowledge

As you become community integrated in your perceptions and plans, consider how you will portray your faith community with its mission to others in a way that preserves your distinctions. Become a student of local and national policies that impact on both communities. Learn about health care reforms, new policies, regulations and their impact on your congregation and the populations you serve:

- The Seniors
- The unemployed
- The youth employed, not in college
- The working poor
- The children
- The disabled and rehabilitated
- The families of the incarcerated
- The families of active and returning soldiers

D. *Learn what is expected in care quality standards for your clients*
   Agencies that monitor care
   Evidence-based Disease Management
   Best Practices and Agency for Research and Healthcare Quality

E. *Learn about Taskforces that may be at work in your community – get involved*
   You can be a spokesperson
   Collaborating to address your concerns
   Gaining support for your programs, getting it adopted by the community at large for the benefit of more

F. *Learn about professional organizations and support group opportunities*

G. *Understand that non-profit organizations and health and human services agencies need you*

_____

One more chapter to go . . . also an important one—about $$$$$

NOTES . . .

Chapter Twelve

GOAL:
Growth Ideas, Sources of Funding, and Strategies of Fund-Raising and Grant Writing

Large Spiritual Communities

It is expected that as a Congregational Nurse practice develops in a congregation, growth will occur, particularly if there is an outreach component. The spiritual community is "home" to individuals and families who seek support in their faith, in family function, in personal challenges. As they gain strength and health wholistically, they draw their network of co-workers, other family, neighbors and friends to the body of believers that influenced change and peace in their lives.

The Congregational Nurse and clergy team should plan for growth and elicit involvement of gifted members in committees that facilitate growth. All facets of church activity should be examined for sensitivity to age, gender, ethnic needs. It is helpful to choose a framework of service to all groups that is expressed in a spiritual thread which helps to communicate goals. Here is an example of one parish that grew rapidly:

Bluestone Parish in the suburbs of a large city has almost 6,000 members with over 3,000 young and middle adult parishioners, 1800 under 21 and 1200 over 65. Before it reached these proportions, the ministry team sought to maintain the closeness and community feeling by forming many small lay-led groups under the direction of 5 ministry teams focusing on worship activities; youth; special groups such as couples, single parents, widows and widowers; education and learning resources; visitation.

Because there were several nurses, a Nursing Cabinet was formed to plan and implement their practice. In congregations where there other health professionals, a multidisciplinary Cabinet may be formed from which teams would work and programs developed. Each health professional or nurse is a member of the ministry teams to give guidance in health-related aspects of service. They may direct other nurses in managing the care of episodic or complex member needs. Taking advantage of every event within a large parish or a large church to promote health becomes the mission of each representative health professional. And the economics of financial support for these positions is easily managed.

Nurses in this setting have excellent opportunity to help lay ministers and clergy understand the physical, emotional, and spiritual deterioration seen in some homes; workshops can be given about vulnerable population needs and family function challenges. The logistics of being able to answer expressed needs among the parishioners was worked out with an emergency call list for nurse duty assignments, regular office hours during the week, regular visitation to shut-ins and families, after-service consultation. With their connection with a health care system, Bluestone Parish was able to form a partnership with the Internal Medicine Residents who paired up with the nurses visiting in homes where a physician was needed.

Small Congregations

In spiritual communities of 150 or less members, the chances of financial support for nursing activities are slim. If there is a nurse who is able by time, energy, or experience to develop a practice, he/she must be dependent on lay volunteers who can be trained to assist in various ways. Perhaps limiting services to one or two ministries dependent on the priority needs of the congregation is most successful—such as the following:

•For those home-bound members who frequent the physician's office and the emergency department of the hospital, a telephone support service by a lay team would allay fears and anxieties centered around their isolation and would improve their quality of life

•Forming inter-generational teams for a feeding program, home repairs, yard work, child care

•Providing a quarterly health presentation at worship service

•Writing a health newsletter for monthly distribution

In rural or suburban areas where congregations may be small, joining together—even in an interfaith coalition—will serve the needs of all efficiently. In urban areas, churches have joined together to address such needs as:

•feeding the homeless,

•cleaning up a decaying neighborhood,

•ministering to those with HIV/AIDS,

•supporting a community health clinic by volunteering,

•establishing information and referral networks for health and human service delivery,

•supporting food banks,

•providing job training programs

•providing adult or child day care

How Does One Fund One or Any of These Ministries?

Time and effort are valuable currency. Volunteers commit those commodities in unselfish ways. Successful programs depend on the caring spirit of those who lead and those who follow and both may be volunteers. But, without a reasonable budget to cover overhead costs, equipment, and promotion, efforts will be diluted eventually in disappointment or regret. Nurses are professionals who, in uncertain economic times, must have at least a stipend with which to maintain credentials and knowledge, and beyond that, to support the cost of living. Faith communities must consider the investment they must make in a health ministry and commit in the long-term to its mission. The funding streams possibly available are:

1. Denominational and interfaith funding sources
2. Health and human services funding sources—local, state, federal
3. Foundations

Consult with the congregation's leaders to learn about funds within the denomination. Search for interfaith programs, such as those mentioned previously, for ideas of fund raising. Local town or cities may have a funding source; the United Way is a good source for small grants to non-profit organizations. At the state level, there are usually foundations to fund health-related needs. Since the early part of this decade, there have been provisions in many federal grants for faith-based organizations. You may learn about what is available at www.grants.gov and in a basic search type in the keyword "faith-based."

The Foundation Directory is the primary resource for catalogued information concerning private foundations in the U.S. You may search at the Washington, DC office or purchase a hard copy of the directory, or purchase access for searches in it online at http://fdonline.foundationcenter.org/ .

This is not a single-handed project. Searching, examining sources and understanding what the eligibility is and what the grantor's expectations are is an intense effort, better done in a team fashion. Then, writing the proposal to satisfy the grantor's requirements is a real challenge. There are several books in the online bookstores that can guide you in this task. There may be an experienced grant writer in your community, certainly, if there is a university there. You will still need to exert your influence in the proposal so that your needs are written in the language of health.

Well, colleague, this is the end of Volume 1 of *"Empowering the Congregational Nurse."* Following this portion of the book are several valuable resources to aid you in establishing a congregational nurse practice and Volume 2 thereafter. My hope is that the information in this book and accompanying volumes are beneficial to you and those who work with you and to those you serve.

My parting thoughts come from Sara Young's little devotional book entitled, *"Jesus Calling."* (Thomas Nelson Publ., 2004). It is based on Scriptural texts of:
Ephesians 3:20-21
Romans 8:6
Isaiah 40:30-31
Revelation 5:13

"I am able to do far beyond all that you ask or imagine. Come to Me with positive expectations knowing that there is no limit to what I can accomplish. Ask My Spirit to control your mind, so that you can think great thoughts of Me. Do not be discouraged by the fact that many of your prayers are yet unanswered. Time is a trainer, teaching you to wait upon Me, to trust Me in the dark. The more extreme circumstances, the more likely you are to see my power and glory at work in the situation. Instead of letting difficulties draw you into worrying, try to view them as setting the scene for My glorious intervention. Keep your eyes and your mind wide open to all that I am doing in your life."

. . . . God

REFERENCES

References are both cited in the chapters and suggested as further sources of information.

Chapter One: Define the Terms and Operationalize Concepts of Health, Community Health and a "healthy community"

Baldwin, J., O'Neil-Conger C., Abegglen J., and HIll, E. (1998). Population-focused and community-based nursing-moving toward clarification of concepts. *Public Health Nursing, 15*(1), 12-18.

Brudenell, I. (2003). Parish Nursing: Nurturing body, mind, spirit, and community. *Public Health Nursing, 20,* (2), 85-94.

Carson, V. (2011). What is the essence of spiritual care? *Journal of Christian Nursing,* July-September, p. 173.

Chase-Ziolek, M. and Iris, M. (2002). Perspectives on the distinctive aspects of providing nursing care in a congregational setting. *Community Health Nursing, 10 (3), 173-186.*

Clark, M. (2008). *Community health nursing: Advocacy for population health.* Upper Saddle River, NJ:Pearson-Prentice Hall Publishers

Levine, M.E. The conservation principles: A retrospective. *Nursing Science Quarterly* (9) 1, Spring, 1996

Long, K. A. The concept of health: Rural perspectives. *Nursing Clinics of North America (28)* 1, 1993; pp. 123-129.

McWilliam, C.L., Stewart, M., Brown, J.B., Desai, K., and Coderre, P. Creating health with chronic illness. *Advanced Nursing Science* (18) 3: pp. 1-15.

Miller, J.F. and Powers, M.J. Development of an instrument to measure hope. *Nursing Research (37)* 1; pp. 6-10.

Nkongho, N. O. The Caring Ability Inventory. In *Measurement of Nursing Outcomes: Self care and coping* (2003) *by* Carolyn Feher Waltz, Ora Lea Strickland, Louise Sherman Jenkins, Colleen Dilorio; Springer Publishers

Otterness, N. , Gehrke, P., and Sener, I. (2007). Partnerships between nursing education and faith communities: Benefits and challenges. *Journal of Nursing Education, 46* (1), 39-44.

Ratner, P. A., Johnson, J.L., and Jeffery, B. Examining emotional, physical, social, and spiritual health as determinants of self-rated health status. *American Journal of Health Promotion* (12)4; pp.275-282.

Schaefer, C., Coyne, J.C., and Lazarus, R.S. The Health-Related Functions of Social Support. *Journal of Behavioral Medicine* (4) 4; pp. 381-405.

Shalala, D. (2010). *The future of nursing: Leading change, advancing health*. Institute of Medicine, Washington, DC.

Simpson, M. and King, M. (1999). "God brought all these churches together": Issues in developing religion-health partnerships in an Appalachian community. *Public Health Nursing, 16* (1), 41-49.

Chapter Two: Define the Terms and Operationalize Concepts of Health Promotion and Self Care

Barton, J.A. Home visitation to migrant farm worker families: An application of Zerwekh's family caregiving model for public health nursing. *Holistic Nursing Practice (9)* 4; pp. 34-40

Chapman, L.S. (1987). Developing a useful perspective on spiritual health: Love, joy, peace and fulfillment. *American Journal of Health Promotion*, Fall, 1987; pp. 12-17.

Clark, M. (2008). *Community health nursing: Advocacy for population health.* Upper Saddle River, NJ:Pearson-Prentice Hall Publishers

McWilliam,. Stewart, Brown, Desai, and Coderre (1996). Creating health with chronic illness. *Advances in Nursing Science (18) 3*

Hawks, S.R., Hull, M. L., Thalman, R. L. , and Richins, P. M. Review of spiritual health: Definition, role, and intervention strategies in health promotion. *American Journal of Health Promotion (9)* 5; pp. 371-378.

Jones, L.C. Measuring guarding: A self-care management process used by individuals with chronic illness. In *Caring and Self-care Measures.* Pp. 58-75.

Ornstein, A. C. & Hunkins, F. P. (1998). (3rd. Ed.) *Curriculum: foundations, principles, and issues.* Boston, MA: Allyn and Bacon.

Padula, C.A. (1992). Self-Care and the Elderly: Review and implications. *Public Health Nursing (9)* 1; pp. 22-28.

Chapter Three: Define and Characterize Congregational Nursing and its Relationship to Community Health

Clark, M. (2008). *Community health nursing: Advocacy for population health.* Upper Saddle River, NJ:Pearson-Prentice Hall Publishers

Duff, V. Spiritual distress: Deciding to care. *Journal of Christian Nursing* (11) 1; pp. 29-31.

Hawks,s., Hull, M., Thalman, R., and Richins, P. (1995). Review of Spiritual Health: Definition, role, and intervention strategies in health promotion. *American Journal of Health Promotion 9* (5), 371-378.

Jackson, J., Clements, P., Averill, J., and Zimbro, K. (2009). Patterns of Knowing: Proposing a theory for nursing leadership. *Nursing Economics$ 27* (3), 149-159.

Kuhn, J. A Profile of Parish Nurses. *Journal of Christian Nursing* (14) 1; pp. 26-28.

Miller, S. and Carson, S. (2010). A documentation approach for Faith Community Nursing. *Creative Nursing 16* 3, p. 122-131.

O'Grady, T. (2011). *Nursing Management,* May, pp. 33-37.

Shalala, D. (2009). A Summary of the December 2009 Forum on the Future of Nursing: Care in the Community. *Institute of Medicine*, Washington, DC.

Solari-Twadell, A. Body, mind, and soul. *Health Progress*, September, 1991; pp. 24-28.

"Doors to Ministry"-- helpful article on how to seize the moment of an open door in an encounter with congregants who have unexpressed needs—in the Appendices

For *operational terms of the health ministries coordinator* and the *nurse in the congregation* refer to the Operations Manual

Chapter Four: The Parish Nurse applies the Nursing Process through role and function

Aroskar, M.A. Community health nurses: Their most significant ethical decision-making problems. *Nursing Cllinics of North America (24)* 4; pp. 967-975.

Broten, P. J. Spiritual care documentation: Where is it? *Journal of Christian Nursing (14)* 2; pp. 29-31

_____ Fundamentals of Parish Nursing at International Parish Nurse Resource Center, viewed August, 2011 at http://parishnurses.org/Fundamentalsofpn.aspx

Purdy, I. (2004). Vulnerable: A concept analysis. *Nursing Forum* 39 *(4), 25-33.*

Schumann, R. Documenting congregational nursing care: A Model. *Journal of Christian Nursing (14)* 2; pp. 32-34.

Simpson, M. and Kind, M. (1999). "God brought all these churches together": Issues in developing religion-health partnerships in an Appalachian community. *Public Health Nursing 16* (1), 41-49.

Trofino, J., Hughes, C., O'Brien, B., Mack, J., Marrinan, M., and Hay, K. (2000). Primary Care Parish Nursing: Academic, service, and parish partnership. *Nursing Administration Quarterly 25* (1), 50-74.

Weis, D., Matheus, R., and Schank, M.J. Health care delivery in faith communities: The Parish Nurse Model. *Public Health Nursing (14)* 6; pp. 368-72.

Wolf, G.A., Boland, S., Aukerman, M. A transformational model for the practice of professional nursing. Part 1. *Journal of Nursing Administration (24)* 4; pp. 51-57.

Ziebarth, D. and Miller, C. (2010). Exploring parish Nurses' perspectives of Parish Nursing training. *Journal of Continuing Education in Nursing 41* (6), 273-80.

Boult, C., Green, A.m Boult, L.m, Pacala, J., Snyder, C. and Leff, B. (2009). Successful models of comprehensive care for older adults with chronic conditions: evidence for the Institute of Medicine's "Retooling for an Aging America" report. *Journal of American Geriatric Society* 57, 2328-2337.

Case Management Society of America, "What is Case Management?" Retrieved on 8/9/2011 at http://www.cmsa.org/Home/CMSA/WhatisaCaseManager/tabid/224/Default.aspx .

Clark, M. (2008). *Community health nursing: Advocacy for population health*. Upper Saddle River, NJ:Pearson-Prentice Hall Publishers

Daley, B.J., and Miller, M. Defining home health care nursing: Implications for continuing nursing education. *The Journal of Continuing Education (27)* 5; pp. 228-237.

Flaskerud, J.H. and Winslow, B.J. Conceptualizing vulnerable populations: Health-related research. *Nursing Research (47)* 2; pp. 69-78.

Hurt, L.W. Care Management: Providing a connecting link. *Nursing Management (26)* 11; 27-33.

Moneyham, L. and Scott, C.B. A model emerges for the community-based nurse care management of older adults. *N&HC: Perspectives on Community (18)* 2; pp. 68-73.

Neal-Boylan, L. (2011). *Clinical case studies in home health care*. Chichester, UK: Wiley-Blackwell.

Osesburg, B, Wynia, K., Middle, B., and Rejneveki, S. (2009). Effects of Case Management for frail older people or those with chronic illness. *Nursing Research* 58 (3), 201-210.

Rheame, A., Frisch, S., Smith, A., and Kennedy, C. Case management and nursing practice. *Journal of Nursing Administration (24)* 3; pp. 30-36.

Robinson, K.M. Family caregiving: Who provides the care, and at what cost? *Nursing Economics (15)* 5; pp. 243-247.

Chapter Six: How a Parish/Congregational Nurse May Blend the Attributes of Both Home Health Nurse and a Case (Care) Manager into the Role

Clark, M. (2008). *Community health nursing: Advocacy for population health*. Upper Saddle River, NJ:Pearson-Prentice Hall Publishers

Sounart, A. (2008). New program treats chronic disease in unconventional clinic. *Nursing News online*, viewed at http://www.nursezone.com/job/MedicalNewsAlerts.asp?articleID=17295&MainCurrent=&SubCurrent=&page=On+the+job&profile=Nursing+news&headline=New+Program+Treats+Chronic+Disease+in+Unconventional+Clinic

Brunner, N.A. That was a good meeting! *Orthopaedic Nursing (12)* 4; pp. 35-39.

Porter-O'Grady, T. The seven basic rules for successful redesign. *Journal of Nursing Administration* (26) 1; pp. 46-53.

Chapter Eight: Building a Force of Volunteers

Bock, K. (1990) *Volunteers: The Hands, Head and Heart of Shepherd's Centers.* Retirement Research Foundation

DiRienzo, S. M. A challenge to nursing: Promoting followers as well as leaders. *Holistic Nursing Practice (9)* 1; pp. 26-30.

_____ *The Lafiya Guide: A Congregational Handbook for Whole-Person Health Ministry,* 1993 Elgin, IL: Association of Brethren Caregivers.

Chapter Nine: Mentoring Active and Would-be Nurses

Andrews M, Chilton F. (2000). Student and mentor perceptions of mentoring effectiveness. *Nurse Education Today 20* (7), 555-62.

Biehl, B. (1996). *Mentoring: confidence in finding a mentor and becoming one.* Nashville, TN: Broadman & Holman Publishers

Busen, N. and Engebretson, J. (1999). Mentoring in Advanced Practice Nursing. *The Internet Journal of Advanced Nursing Practice 2* (2).

Espina-Gabriel P. (2002). Journey to professional transformation: a mentoring experience. *Seminar Nurse Management 10*(3), 140-2; discussion 142-3.

Fingeld-Connett, D. (2008). Qualitative comparison and synthesis of nursing presence and caring. *International Journal of Nursing Terminologies and classifications 19* (3), p. 111-119.

Hofmann P, and Noblin J. (2002). Mentoring dialogue: critical questions and answers. *Healthcare Executive 17*(6), 8-13.

Liang B, Tracy A, Taylor C, and Williams L. (2002). Mentoring college-age women: a relational approach. *American Journal of Community Psychology 30* (2), 271-88.

Marquis, B. and Huston, C. (2006). Leadership roles and management functions in nursing, (5th Ed.), p. 390-1, Philadelphia, PA: Lippincott Williams & Wilkins Publ.

Martucci M. (1999). Jesus: Our mentoring model. Journal of Christian Nursing *16* (2), 30.

Mentoring Issue. (2002). *Creative Nurse 8* (3), 13-4.

Morris E, and Burggraf V. (2001). A mentoring relationship. Two-nurses grow in faith & knowledge. *Journal of Christian Nursing18*(1), 29-30

Moscinski P. (2002). Take charge of your mentoring experience. *Healthcare Executive* 17 (4), 62.

Murray R. (2002). Mentoring. Perceptions of the process and its significance. *Journal Psychosocial Nursing Mental Health Service 40* (4), 44-51.

Nelms B. (2001). Mentoring: promoting a legacy for the future. *Journal Pediatric Health Care 15*(4), 159-60.

Orpeza, N. (2009). Perspectives on mentoring. *Advance for Nurses,* Feb. 9, p. 7.

Parker D. (2002). A workshop on mentoring across gender and culture lines. *Academy of Medicine 77* (5), 461.

Parse R. (2002). Mentoring moments. *Nursing Science Quarterly 15* (2), 97.

Shaffer B, Tallarico B, and Walsh J. (2000). Win-win mentoring. *Dimensions of Critical Care Nursing 19* (3), 36-8.

Schmidt K. (1999). Mentoring. Sharing our wisdom. *Journal of Christian Nursing 16* (2), 27-9.

Simmons C. (2002). Make a difference with mentoring. *Critical Care Nurse 22*(3), 20.

Sitzman, K. (1998). Mentoring. *Home Healthcare Nurse 16* (1), p. 20.

Snelson C, Martsolf D, Dieckman B, Anaya E, Cartechine K, Miller B, Roche M, Shaffer J. (2002). Caring as a theoretical perspective for a nursing faculty mentoring program. *Nurse Education Today 22*(8), 654-60.

Snyder, M. (1995). "Becoming": A method for expanding systemic thinking and deepening empathic accuracy. *Family Process 34,* June, p. 241-253.

Velazquez-Marsh L. (1999). Both sides learn through mentoring. *ONS News 14*(12), 7.

Verdejo T. (2002). Mentoring: a model method. *Nursing Management 33* (8), 15-6.

Weston M. (2001). Leading into the future: coaching and mentoring Generation X employees. *Seminar Nurse Management 9* (3), 157-60.

Wills C. and Kaiser L. (2002). Navigating the course of scholarly productivity: the protege's role in mentoring. *Nursing Outlook 50* (2), 61-6.

Chapter Ten: Strategies for Promoting and Building a Health Promotion Initiative

Brunet, D., Plaut, A., Wolf, S., Huo, D., Solomon, M., Dekayie, G., Quinn, M., Lipton, R., Chin, M. (2011). Reach-Out: A family based diabetes prevention program for African American youth. *Journal of the National Medical Association 103* (3), 269-277.

CDC.gov. Pages regarding sexually transmitted disease statistics for 2009.

Cornelius, J. (2009). The birds, the bees, and the Bible: single African American mothers' perceptions of a faith-based sexuality education program. *Journal of Cultural Diversity 16* (1), 21-25.

Glanz, K., Lewis, F. M., Rimer, B. K., (1997). (Eds., 2nd Ed.). *Health behavior and health education: Theory, research, and practice.* San Francisco, CA:Jossey-Bass Publisher

Hawkins, S. (2010). Improving glycemic control in older adults using a videophone motivational diabetes self-management intervention. *Research and Theory for Nursing Practice: an International Journal, 24* (4), 217-232.

Hurley, J. and Mohnkern, S. (2004). Mobilize support groups to meet congregational needs. *Journal of Christian Nursing 21* (4) 34-39.

Johnstone, B., Yoon, D., Rupright, J., and Reid-Arndt, S. (2009). Relationships among spiritual beliefs religious practices, congregational support and health for individuals with traumatic brain injury. *Brain Injury 23* (5), 411-129.

Maiback, E. and Parrett, R. L. (1995). *Designing health messages.* Thousand Oaks, CA:Sage

Perkins, E. R., Simnett, I., and Wright, L.(1999). *Evidence-based health promotion.* New York: Wiley & Sons.

Rainey, J. and Lindsay G. 101 questions for community health promotion program planning. *Journal of Health Education 25* (5), 309-312.

Rew, L. and Bowman, K. (2008). Protecting youth from early and abusive sexual experiences. *Pediatric Nursing 34* (1), 19-26.

Weber, M. (2010). The importance of exercise for individuals with chronic mental illness. *Journal of Psychosocial Nursing 48* (10), 35-40.

Chapter Eleven: Understand the Value of Interfaith Collaboration; How to Build Effective Relationships and Partnerships in the Community

Ross, A., King, N., and Firth, J. (2005). Inter-professional relationships and collaborative working: encouraging reflective practice. *Online Journal of Issues in Nursing 10* (1).

Simpson, M. and King, M. (1999). "God Brought all These Churches Together": Issues in developing religion-health partnerships in an Appalachian community. *Public Health Nursing 16* (1), 41-49.

Weinstein, S. (2004). Strategic partnerships: Bridging the Collaboration Gap. *Journal of Infusion Nursing 27* (5), 297-301.

Chapter Twelve: Learn Sources of Funding and Strategies of Fund-raising and Grant Writing

Carlson, M., and O'Neal-McElrath, T. (2008). *Winning grants step by step.* The Alliance for Non-Profit Management, San Francisco, CA: Jossey-Bass.

APPENDICES to Empower the Leader

A. Spiritual Gifts Module

B. Practice Development Worksheet

C. Practice Models of Care

D. Congregational Nurse Practice Model Designs

E. Brief Strategic Plan

F. Doors to Ministry in Pastoral Conversations

G. Community Senior Wellness Management Program

H. Stories and Scenarios

SPIRITUAL GIFTS
A Study of Their Relationship to the Congregational Nurse

PURPOSE: To conduct the student through an exploration of Scripture and the writings of selected authors concerning the spiritual Gifts God has given each subject of His creation and to assist the student in identifying those gifts. It is suggested that the student begin this study with prayer for enlightenment.

THE CHURCH IS: The fellowship of believers

WHO   1. Share the divine life of Christ.

2. Participate in individual and corporate growth.

3. Are becoming like Christ.

4. Are gaining the victory over sin.

5. Build up one another.

6. Are examples of the "process" not the "product" of salvation.

THE LAYMAN IS: The member of the body of Christ

WHO   1. Is growing in Christ.

2. Is ordained to minister and to serve.

3. Is an example of the process.

DEFINING SPIRITUAL GIFTS

Talents	**and**	**Spiritual Gifts**
1. Are naturally inherited developed by the Holy Spirit		1. Are endowed and empowered and
2. Are of benefit to the individual and mankind within society on a social level		2. Are of benefit to the individual and mankind in the church on the spiritual level

NOTE: Talents and spiritual gifts are:

Not synonymous, nor mutually exclusive

God can consecrate and empower a talent and thus make it a gift.

Describing Spiritual Gifts   -   I Corinthians 12:4-31

What is the Source of Spiritual Gifts?   *The Holy Spirit, Jesus promised before He as-*
cended to Heaven - John 14; Luke 11:13

What is the function and purpose of   *Acts 1:8*
Spiritual Gifts?   *Acts of the Apostles, Ch. 1-5.*

NOTE: Spiritual Gifts are bestowed by the Holy Spirit, not through election procedures to office status, not just to church leaders, not by church assignment.

How is control maintained over   *2Timothy 1:11-14; Isaiah 8:20;*
Spiritual Gifts?   *I Corinthians 14:32,37; 15:1,2*

NOTE: Spiritual Gifts are governed by the revealed Word of God and must be exercised within the boundaries set by the Scriptures.

The New Testament presents Spiritual Gifts as operational tools for ministry in the church. Passages in Romans, I Corinthians, Ephesians, and I Peter describe or allude to 27 gifts. They are defined by their function. Gifts that are assigned an individual by the Holy Spirit are the framework for one's lifelong ministry in the church. They are "promised to every believer according to his need for the Lord's work." (The Desire of Ages, p 823.) Results of their function are only limited by the degree of commitment to discipleship and response to the Lord's call one possesses.

Spiritual Gifts are given to advance the kingdom of God   **I Peter 4:10**

Principles implied:

1. Priority in exercising gifts is driven by the urgency of the times

2. The gift-holder is accountable for their use

3. Gifts should be used with authority because they come from God

4. The exercise of Spiritual Gifts should bring honor and glory to God

5. God should receive the credit for their use.

What recurrent theme is associated with Spiritual Gifts?   **I Corinthians 12**

Romans 12

The universal gift - LOVE   **I Corinthians 13**

I John 3:11-24

Love is essential to the theme of UNITY. Love initiates the development of a Christian personality that should possess all of what Paul calls "fruit of the Spirit."

Love	
Joy	The Triad of Experience
Peace	

Faithfulness	
Meekness	The Triad of Conduct
Self-control	

Long suffering	
Gentleness	The Triad of Character
Goodness	

Galatians 5:22-23

Spiritual Gifts are the <u>result of the Spirit working "through" us,</u>

Fruit of the Spirit are the <u>result of the Spirit working "in" us.</u>

Spiritual Gifts of Ministry

<u>Supportive gifts:</u>

Helps and mercy   Acts 9:25-27; Matthew 25:24-40

The gift of "helps" is a special ability to invest talents and energy in the life and ministry of other members of the body, by taking on tasks that may be menial, without seeking credit, just for the joy of doing them.

"Mercy" is a special gift to feel genuine empathy and compassion for others, both believers and non-believers, who suffer distressing physical, emotional, mental, or social problems. Compassion is translated into deeds of comfort.

Exhortation and Encouragement   Acts 4:36; 9:27; 14:23; 15:37-39

"Exhortation" is a special ability to speak words in season of comfort, consolation, encouragement, and counsel.

Giving and Hospitality   I Corinthians 4; Luke6:38; 2 Corinthians 9:7; I Peter 4:9

<u>Teaching gifts:</u>

Teaching   Acts 19:8-10; I Timothy 3:1,2; 4:11-14; 2 Timothy 2:1,2

Special God-given ability to communicate information, attitudes, and skills relevant to the health and ministry of the body and its members in such a way that others will learn.

Knowledge   Matthew 13:11; 2 Corinthians 2:14; 4:13; I Timothy 2:4; 2 Peter 3:18

The God-given gift to discover, accumulate, analyze, and clarify information and ideas, particularly as they relate to the church and the well-being of the body.

Wisdom   Ecclesiastes 12:11; Proverbs 9:10; Exodus 31:1-6

The ability to make decisions and solve problems based on knowledge and experience, particularly as it relates to the influence of the Holy Spirit.

Pastoring and Shepherding   I Peter 5:1-3 (shared meaning with office)

Assuming a long-term personal responsibility for the spiritual welfare of a group of believers. May also include discipling.

<u>Leadership and Administrative gifts:</u>

Servant-Leadership   Matthew 20:20-28; I Timothy 5:17; John 13:35; Mark 9:33-35; Romans 12:3, 10; I Peter 5:3; Ephesians 5:21

Ability to set goals within God's purpose and to communicate these goals in such a way that members voluntarily and harmoniously work for the glory of God.

Apostleship   Acts 9:15,16

Means "someone who is sent." Frontline pioneers who have a strong sense of God's call to establish new missions, a forceful personality that trusts in God in whatever circumstance, has multiple gifts, courage.

Administration   I Corinthians 12:28

Ability to understand short- and long-range goals and to effectively develop and execute plans for their accomplishment within God's will.

Faith   I Corinthians 12;9

Ability to discern and accept with extraordinary confidence the will and purposes of God.

Application to Nursing Practice

Based on the above study, a correlation can be drawn to nursing practice. The role of the nurse harmonizes with the concept of Spiritual Gifts in this way:

- The nurse is a caregiver utilizing special gifts   Galatians 5:22,23

- The nurse is a professional in excellence   2 Peter 1:3-11

- The nurse is a facilitator of unity, harmony   I Corinthians 12; John 17; Ephesians 2:11-22; 4:3; Romans 12

- The nurse is a teacher/educator/evangelist for health   Romans 12; I Corinthians 12; Ephesians 4; Acts 19:8-10

- The nurse holds a magnitude of responsibility   James 3:1

- The nurse is a researcher using wisdom, knowledge, discovery of truth   2 Corinthians 2:14; Ephesians 4:13; Matthew 13:11

•The nurse is a problem solver using wisdom	Proverbs 9:10
•The Parish Nurse is a pastor/shepherd	I Peter 5:1-3
•The nurse practices leadership	Matthew 20:27; Acts 5:17; Romans 12:3,8; Acts 7:10; 15:13-21; Hebrews 13:17; Luke 9:1

•The nurse practices gifts of support

The Model for Expressing/Teaching Spiritual Gifts   Deuteronomy 11:18-21

1. Receive words and impressions from God into the mind

2. Bind them as a sign on the hands to represent tasks dedicated to God's will and on

the forehead (frontals) to represent a mind dedicated to God's will

3. Teach them to the children (or others) throughout every activity from morning to night

4. Write them on the doorpost of the home as a symbol to the neighbors of dedication to God's will

5. Write them on the gates to your property, where contact is made with the community, to symbolize dedication to God's will

The Benefits of Understanding and Using Your Spiritual Gifts

•They help in setting life's priorities

•They direct you in God's will and in finding self-fulfillment

•They help control feelings of guilt and inadequacies

•They strengthen self-image and help in self-acceptance

•They identify an area for study and self-development

•They help you find recognition in society

On the next page is an Inventory to help you discover your gifts . . . .

Gift of Exhortation

(Please circle)

Yes **No** Do people often tell you that what you said to them was a real help and comfort?

Yes **No** Do you desire to counsel effectively the perplexed, the guilty, or the addicted?

Yes **No** Do you find that you seem to be easy to talk; people engage in heart-to-heart talk?

Yes **No** Do you find yourself speaking words of encouragement to those who are troubled, discouraged and uncertain?

Yes **No** Do you often correct someone's view with solid scriptural counsel and find that people take your counsel?

Gift of Teaching

(Please circle)

Yes **No** Do you enjoy teaching the Bible and find that people learn from your teaching?

Yes **No** Do you enjoy spending considerable time learning Bible truth so that you can communicate it to others?

Yes **No** Do you usually organize biblical information in a careful and systemic way so that listeners clearly understand it?

Yes **No** Have you read the Bible through a number of times?

Yes **No** Given a choice, do you prefer biblical passages that are rich in doctrine?

Gift of Pastoring

(Please circle)

Yes **No** Do you enjoy spending time nurturing and caring for others?

Yes **No** Have you been instrumental in helping some people return to the Lord?

Yes **No** Can you affirm that your Christian example has influenced a group of Christians?

Yes **No** Are you considered by people in your church to be a spiritual leader?

Yes **No** Do you tend to provide guidance for the whole person--relationally, emotionally spiritually, and theologically?

Gift of Leadership

(Please circle)

Yes	**No**	Do people seem to listen and agree when you speak with them?
Yes	**No**	Do people tend to believe in you and follow your leadership?
Yes	**No**	Do people accept the goals you suggest?
Yes	**No**	Do you often end up as the leader of groups you join?
Yes	**No**	Do things go smoothly when you are in charge?

Gift of Administration

(Please circle)

Yes	**No**	Do people recognize your ability to organize ideas, people, and activities?
Yes	**No**	Is it easy for you to make plans, set goals and organize ways and means of accomplishing them?
Yes	**No**	Do you tend to organize unorganized activities almost automatically?
Yes	**No**	Are you usually able to get people to do things without a lot of persuasion or pressure?
Yes	**No**	Do you enjoy being assigned a task and then carrying it out in an organized way?

After discovering what your Spiritual Gifts are, they may be verified by:

1. Agreement of some or all of the church body or professional group with your findings.
2. Through intercessory prayer of others, ask the Lord to confirm your gifts.
3. Use your gifts in ministry--exercise them. With use they will mature.

NOTE: "A restless, growing conviction is often the first sign that God is endowing you with a combination of gifts necessary to meet a need in the church and in your profession. A specific call by the Lord to a ministry will inevitably be accompanied by the gifts that will make that ministry effective, provided a person's motivation and attitude follow biblical guidelines and principles."

The end of the author's contribution; the beginning of yours . . .

References:

Zackrison, J. W. Spiritual Gifts: Keys to Ministry. Adult Sabbath School Quarterly, 1st Quarter, 1997. Sabbath School/Personal Ministries Department, General Conference of Seventh-day Adventists.

Naden, R. Your Spiritual Gifts: Making the Great Discovery. (1989). Berrien Springs, MI. Finding Your Spiritual Gifts: Wagner-Modified Houts Questionaire

I. INTRODUCTION

A. Description of Service (overview of spiritual community-wider community-nurse relationship; some demographics of community, of church; preparation of Parish Nurse/Nurse team; perceived boundaries of scope and practice.)

B. Purpose

C. Objectives (At least 3)

D. Mutually-defined Mission

II. CONCEPTUAL FRAMEWORK FOR SERVICE

A. Philosophy/Ethos

B. History

III. ORGANIZATION STRUCTURE AND FUNCTION

A. Overall Role and Development of Practice

· Health Committee/Health Board member representation, its role and function in relationship to Congregational Nurse practice/program.

· Fiscal support structures to sustain practice (stipend, salary, operating budget)

· Contracts, agreements, insurance arrangements

· Office and equipment provision

· Other expenses such as travel, phone

· Communication pathways re care activities; division and joint responsibilities with clergy, others

B. Service Role and Activities of Congregational Nurse

1. Role

2. Model of Practice

3. Activities (boundaries/limitations; degree of autonomy)

C. Description of Programs and Services

1. Programs (usually health promotional; include tools and procedures used, guidelines for each program, contact people, scripts for presentations, etc.)

2. Services (caregiving, counseling, etc.)

3. Documentation tools: recordkeeping, communication, assessments and plans, outcomes measurement tools, referral forms, etc.

Practice Models of Care

This collection is intended to provide concepts of practice that might be used to begin incrementally while gaining increasing support or for efforts limited by time or other resources based on what others have been doing and what is possible to create.

SMALL STEPS TO TRUST AND CREDIBILITY-BUILDING

After-services Screening

Blood pressure checks are a common opener to building trust and availability with the congregants.

After-services Consultation ("The Nurse is in – 5 cents")

Opening the nurse's office or another small room for privacy and inviting those with problems or concerns to explain their need in a few minutes and making an appointment for a later meeting or a home visit. The 5 cents requirement may not only place some value on the encounter, but may also "break the ice" with humor in an anxiety-laden moment.

After-services Appetizer

If it is the custom to offer beverages as a social "glue" after services, set up a table offering a small serving of a healthy beverage (fruit smoothie from blender, vegetable blend drink, tofu milk, banana shake, etc.) and/or a healthy cracker. Provide a little attractive card stating nutritional value and the recipe.

POPULATION FOCUS – By Age

Youth

Join the Youth Ministry Team to promote health through interactive video presentations, health-based theatrical play presentations, health fairs, reaching out ministries to peers in community

Young Adults & Young Parents

Serve as a consultant and health promotion expert on health-related topics of sexuality, relationships, nurturing children, avoiding disease and injury by reducing risk-taking activities, self-care strategies, optimal family planning, and assuming responsibility for caregiving of all ages, etc. Recruit and train volunteers to conduct:

Pregnancy Support Ministry	Career Enhancement in God's Will Support Group
Welcome Baby	Financial Management Seminars or Support
Kitchen Table Moms	Fatherhood Support
Parenting Support & Seminars	Teen Health
Parent-Teacher Support Group	

Older Adults

Serve as consultant and educator in the areas of "sandwich generation" issues, stress of career changes and other work-related problems, optimizing health through diet, weight control, relaxation and trust methods, quitting substance abuse, wise use of prescription and OTC medications, relationships, adjusting to aging, financial planning for the future, careplanning for the future, etc.

Elderly

Serve as an advocate for their increasing needs related to: self-care, injury prevention, mobility, management of diseases and conditions, decreasing family support, housing, safety, interaction with other health professionals, social stimulation, domestic assistance, independence changes, mental health/depression alleviation, financial survival, substance abuse. Organize volunteer services to help them maintain optimal independence in the community. Some programs might be:

Widow-to-Widow Friendship Groups	Specialized support groups for older women
Seniors Teaching Seniors	Mall-Walking groups
Senior-to-Senior Telephone Support	Voice-mail Program as Medication Time Reminder

POPULATION FOCUS – BY ETHNICITY OR CULTURE

Work with races or ethnic groups different from your own in your congregation to assure culturally-sensitive health promotion and disease management resources. Build programs around health concerns that are specific for those populations, such as hypertension in African-American males, obesity in Latinos, etc. Recognize acculturation difficulties of other groups when planning health promotion events and educational approaches for Caucasians and desiring to be inclusive.

POPULATION FOCUS – BY SOCIOECONOMIC FACTORS

Both within the congregation and in the community beyond there may be hidden tragedies brought on my poverty or marginalization of society. Developing programs of nutrition and feeding, housing, friendly visits, etc. requires a "healthy" congregation in order to reach into or out to such comprehensive and complex problems.

Some Examples of Specialty Congregational Nurse Ministries

IN-REACHING PROGRAMS

Family Preservation

While promoting family health among congregants generally, families with problems or are dysfunctional are identified and worked with more intensely, bringing in counseling experts if necessary. Those parents/caregivers of children who have been reported to authorities and families whose children have gotten into trouble through substance abuse, violence, etc. may be candidates for a congregational team prepared to intervene and strengthen the family structure and function. (Check with state/local child welfare system)

Intergenerational Connection

Volunteers recruited from children 10-19 can be trained for tasks forces of household, yard, and personal assistance activities:

•In Summer essential yard work and home repairs; smoke detector installment, home safety assessments

•In Winter in the North, snow shoveling, grocery shopping and delivery, checking for adequate heat

•Anytime, Friendly Visits focused on expressed needs of elders

•Paired teams of a youth and an Senior to motivate and lead a group of Seniors in exercise activities

•Youth teaching Seniors about computers; Seniors giving Youth history lessons from personal experience

Mobility Programs for Seniors and Disabled

Training volunteers (or using health professionals as volunteers) to bring a walking program into the home of sedentary Seniors and disabled persons to strengthen their mobility ability. The two-times-a-week visits give opportunity to teach family or other caregivers, assess the Senior for depression, nutrition status, assess the home for safety, make proper referrals, report to physician progress. Delays institutionalization.

A **Foot Care Program** designed to assess, educate about care, and monitor status is a wonderful service for Seniors and those with chronic health problems that compromise circulation and skin integrity. This can extend into an outreach program (see below).

Grief-Loss Support

In congregations where the majority are attending and non-attending elderly, emphasis on loss, its meaning to life, coping, optimizing abilities, and applying spiritual insights may be the main focus of service by the congregational nurse. But in all congregations at some time or another, grief-loss support and intervention is essential.

Hopeful Interventions

Performing depression assessments on home-bound individuals and/or their caregivers as well as other more ambulatory members of the congregation offers an opportunity for individual or group interventions of discussion centered around messages of Hope found in Scripture (Jeremiah 29:11).

Welcome Baby Program

A visitation program connects volunteer members with parents of a new baby. Monthly visits are made to deliver a milestone booklet on growth and development, parent's concerns, and spiritual encouragement. A helping relationship is formed over the course of a year. Other child programs in the spiritual community can extend this influence. An excellent outreach opportunity as well.

OUTREACH PROGRAMS

Health Screening and Follow-up Using Students

Nursing and other health sciences college students are eager to work with community programs. Scheduling screenings and health fairs to coincide with their availability offers an excellent collaborative experience. They then can follow-up with health and self-care teaching to clients/members served.

After School Programs

A church may establish a partnering relationship with a school in the nearby community in order to offer health education after school in the afternoons; may also serve as a service for latch-key children if expanded to include other activities.

Teen Link (Durham, NC.)

Several churches together formed an initiative to reach teens of the community called "Teen Link" wherein selected members were trained as Adult Resource Persons (ARP's) to provide health education. Training focused on teen issues such as adolescent development, sexuality, substance abuse, community resources, working with groups, and how to connect with church activities.

Fatherhood Program

The March of Dimes and Alpha Fraternity developed a unique educational project that helps young men learn about their role in responsible child rearing. An excellent opportunity for congregational health ministries and the Parish Nurse.

Prison Health Ministry

Bringing health promotion that is culturally sensitive and focused on restoring God's image in imprisoned populations has potential for decreasing recidivism and improving prison behavior.

Partnering with Community Agencies

Provide health assessments and health education programs to individuals in public housing through the Housing Authority agency. Delivering Meals on Wheels for the Aging Services Agency and follow-up with attention to other needs of those individuals is also needed.

Foot Clinic

Assessment of feet for skin integrity, circulation, deformities, nail problems, etc. is an excellent service for Senior Centers and other gatherings. Health promotion and a spiritual lesson of "Walking in His Steps" enriches this outreach.

A "Super Pantry" Approach

Offering nutritional workshops to lower-income families in a mentoring method will also elicit interest in the extended community so that nutritional assessments may be made and education of the workshop becomes more inclusive in a neighborhood.

Congregational Nursing Practice Designs

IOWA (Individuals of Wholistic Awareness)

The Parish Nurse opens a consultation service with members whereby each participant attends a health promotion series of presentations; meets with the PN personally and completes a Health Risk Assessment; sets personal goals and meets regularly with PN for support and guidance.

Division of Nursing Service

In large congregations where there are several nurses, individual service focus can be formed with each nurse responsible to selected populations, e.g. a Foster Grandparent program where one or more take responsibility for frail elderly, another may provide care and planning for the disabled.

Nurse Team Model

Two or more nurses in a congregation develop the practice together and share activities according to the particular skills of each. If several nurses participate, a Coordinator or Director is chosen.

Nurse-Clergy Team Model

The nurse in the congregation and the pastor or clergy form a health ministry team in which they share health care institution visiting, home visiting, meetings and services (any degree of those). They may share it by the factors of age, gender, ethnicity, geography of the population of members.

Nurse-Clergy-Physician Team

An ideal situation in which the Parish Nurse, the minister/clergy/pastor include either a selected physician from the congregation or the member's physician or both in a visiting and counseling team.

Consortium of Congregations

One nurse may serve 3-4 church congregations, receiving a stipend or salary from the consortium. Larger consortia require more nurses who may work as a team in varying configurations.

Consortium of Congregations & Health Care Facilities

Hospitals, rehabilitation centers, or long-term care facilities may partner with churches in the area served and sponsor one or more Parish Nurses to minister to the members in those churches and/or non-churched individuals in the service area. Benefits and insurance are usually paid by the healthcare facility and the salary may be jointly provided. Merit raises should also be given. Performance evaluation and continuing education is usually provided by the health care facility.

Partnering of the Church with Academia

A church-based, nurse-managed wellness resource center staffed with the Parish Nurse and individuals of expertise from an educational institution. Satellite outreach clinics can be held in one or more churches, preparing volunteers from that membership.

Brief Strategic Plan for Pine Tree Valley Church
Health Ministries (An Example)
January 2019

Human Resources of the Pine Tree Valley Church

All health personnel, active and retired, comprising MD's, nurses, dentists, dental hygienists, health educators, chiropractors, physician's assistant, social worker, certified nursing assistants, physical/occupational therapy, pharmacy technician (and others I may not know about).

Thus far I have 40 names.

Purpose

To develop a Health Council from which to accomplish the following Mission:

Mission and Subsequent Goals

1. To advance the discipling role of the church and its members by building health literacy and the awareness of the significance of practicing a healthful lifestyle in preparation for the work of the Holy Spirit

Goal 1: Health literacy through these strategies:

    a. Printed materials for distribution in a dedicated literature rack on a church hallway

    b. A/V media for distribution and teaching and support needs from a monitored library

    c. Establishment of a "Health Emphasis Sabbath" (quarterly) during which 20 minutes is devoted to health education and/or a health seminar is presented in the afternoon

        1. Scripts are written for small groups to emphasize health

        2. Health presentations and A/V materials are provided for children and youth Schools
with   health council members presenting

2. To increase knowledge about disease and accident prevention and health promoting practices individually and in families.

Goal 1: Programming across the life span through these strategies:

    a.   Assuring current sources for knowledge-seekers with website links and printed guides to

local, state, and national organizations

    b. A Home safety program for elders and other semi-dependent people (home assessment, teaching, and repairs)

    c. Child health and development and parenting workshops

    d. Women's health and men's health education and screening with cooperation of their primary health care providers

Goal 2: To educate/prepare lay health advisors who can work in their communities

Goal 3: To educate members in emergency preparedness and disaster response

Goal 4: To establish a school health "clinic" for both elementary and high school the church owns for prevention and health promotion education

3. To assist members in managing disease states and conditions and accessing health care as necessary.

Goal 1: Case finding and surveillance through these strategies:

a. Regularly scheduled screening programs for mini-assessments – Vital Signs, BMI and weight management, hearing and vision, blood sugar, etc.

b. Professional home visits supplemental to the Home Safety Program

4. To build community among church health professionals and opportunity for professional and spiritual growth in the context of health and practice.

Goal 1: Schedule regular education and health planning sessions for Health Council members

Goal 2: Equip health professionals and health associates in team skills and teaching resources

Goal 3: Expect that all Health Council members assume at least one role in health promotion and intervention

5. To extend the wealth of resources on health and the intent of their application beyond church membership to at least the local community. The following are goals toward that.

Goal 1: Space has be assigned in the church building for operations (confidential office space, computer, phone; eventually a classroom)

Goal 2: A bridge will be developed to the House of Clay for off-site activities such as:

a. Screening clinics

b. An Alcohol Addiction support group service

c. Regularly scheduled, periodic addiction recovery seminars on tobacco, substance abuse, gambling, pornography, and internet misuse, overeating

d. Partner with the Spanish church on community health promotion at HOC

Goal 3: Partnerships will be developed with community agencies and church members will be prepared to volunteer with such groups as:

Hillside County

a. First Step & CASA (domestic abuse)   b. Hand-in-Hand (pregnant teens)

c. Meals on Wheels   d. Free clinic

Pendleton County

a. Healthy Start (early childhood)   b. Free clinic c. Concern Hotline   d. The Jails

Possible Outcomes

1. Multidisciplinary service and education teams

2. A faith nursing practice that includes volunteer training and supervision in its functions

3. Outreach to secular community and provision of programs and services to other churches

4. Modeling the health professions to children and youth of the church and the schools

(Melody Firestone, RN, MPH, MSN; Health Ministries Director)

Doors to Ministry in Pastoral Conversations

By A. Keith Ethridge, M.Div.
(with a verbatim by Chaplain (LCDR) David C. Cromer, USN)

The art of pastoral visitation or pastoral conversation is one of the most neglected topics in theological education. This is tragically ironic since hardly a day passes in our lives as ministers that we do not find ourselves sitting face-to-face with a hurting soul, praying to find the best way to be helpful. The art of pastoral conversation depends upon the minister's ability to recognize and appropriately respond to the pastoral opportunities, or "doors to ministry," that present themselves in dialogue with parishioners during any given moment in time. Doors to ministry appear and are gone in an instant. Many factors influence a minister's ability to see these "doors to ministry" and to respond in helpful ways that are experienced as pastoral care. More often, the restraining factors or barriers that prevent the minister from moving through these doors to ministry exist within his/her own unconscious self.

So, how can we better prepare ourselves to see these doors to ministry in the midst of our pastoral visitation? What process can we use to discover the barriers within our unconscious and transform or convert them from barriers to resources for ministry? It must involve an intensive self-reflective process. It must involve our willingness to look at unresolved issues from our past, particularly our relationships within our family of origin. We must look at our own personal development and family of origin within the larger context of what we know about family systems, human personality development, and social behavior. We must integrate this with what we theologically know about what it means to be created in the image of God; what it means to "be" in this world with other human beings; and what it means to live with law and grace.

(Chaplain A. Keith Ethridge was Commandant of Chaplain Education and Development Center for the United States Department of Veterans Affairs Chaplain Service in 2012.)

Goals:

1. Optimize Functional Capacity

    A. Mobility

        1) Walking Senior Program

        2) Transportation initiatives (community coalitions)

        3) Neighborhood/local community recreation activities

        4) Organized competition sports

        5) Year-round day trips for culture, learning, recreation

        6) Wellness Center activities

        7) Volunteerism

        8) Cross-generational activities

    B. Integrity of Senses

        1) Regular vision/hearing screenings in all communities

        2) Patient education

    C. Mental/thinking Integrity

        1) Computer literacy at community sites & churches

2. Optimize Quality of Life (QOL)

    A. Connections of Hope programs

    B. Collaborative case finding: NP's, PN's, HH, Hospice, Dept. Social Services, Public Health Department

    C. Community ElderCare Alliance/Collaborative Initiatives

    D. Collaboration with support groups

3. Prevent Disease

    A. Education

        1) Computer access

        2) Group teaching

        3) Empowerment to self-care and looking out for each other

        4) Telephone health education library

    B. Adequate nutrition programs

    C. Environmental safety measures

        1) Home inspection & repairs

2) Community control of crime, other disasters

   D. Immunization programs

   E. Psychosocial support resources

   F. Education

   G. Regular monitoring: MD's, NP's, PN's, HH

4. Detect Diseases Early

   A. Regular screenings: Hypertension, Cholesterol, Vision & Hearing, Nutrition, depression & memory loss, Cancer, Thyroid, Osteoporosis, blood sugar, anemia

   B. Mobile Clinic Services

   C. Advice Line

5. Optimized Disease Management by Seniors

Stories and Scenarios

Congregational Nursing and the work of trained volunteers is seen as a wholistic approach to augmenting and extending acute and in-home health care services and to managing chronic conditions. By reaching those unconnected to communities of faith and limited in resources for self-care, Connections of Hope determines to widen the net of support for health and human services.

Mr. Good is an elderly gentleman living in a subsidized apartment in town who is frequently rushed to the emergency room for episodic health problems due to emphysema and compromised circulation. He has been a smoker for over 40 years and, because of the loss of sensation in his legs, he often injures them. The sores heal very slowly and some do not. He has just been discharged after several weeks of home health care services for this reason. Reduced circulation to his brain at times causes him to become dizzy, sometimes black out and fall--this is when he rushed to the emergency room.

He has a son in the area who lives with his family on his small farm in the country. They seem to be involved in their own problems and don't visit very much. The relationship has not been good for several years, so it is not possible to live with them-even if they had room. Mr. Good is lonely and depressed and only ventures out of his apartment to go to the nearby convenience store to buy food.

At his last visit to the E.R., the nurse referred his case to a Community-based Parish Nurse. Amy McDaniel visits him at home. She is not surprised at the mess she finds because she is familiar with circumstances and needs of the elderly. The cupboards and refrigerator hold foods of poor nutritional quality. Cleaning and restored order are badly needed.

Amy learns that he has once been a member of the church she serves. Over the next few weeks Amy is able to obtain volunteers to clean the apartment on a regular basis and involve Mr. Good in the activity as he is able. These become ties for conversation and spiritual restoration. Other volunteers are assigned to take him to appointments with a physician on a regular basis and to the bank and grocery store where they help him choose nutritious foods. Funds are obtained from his son for an emergency alert system and a neighbor is taught how to monitor his safety from day to day.

RURAL STORIES

1. Mountain Valley Retreat has a high incidence of alcohol-related automobile accidents involving teenage drivers. In the past 2 years since 2 Congregational Nurses started programs in their churches, the concept of nurses leading in congregational health has gained ground in 2 other churches. The local hospital's community outreach department has assisted all the PNs to form a coalition to which Public Health nurses have joined. After 6 months of planning together and seeking opinion and expertise from the academic community and parent groups, a comprehensive educational program is developed with the following components: -surveillance of alcohol vendors within 25 miles of the community
--better organized and increased youth recreational activities that include teens as participants
--improvement in educational programs in the middle, junior high, and high schools
--cooperate with law enforcement officers who identify repeat offenders
--establish parent seminars and support groups

How would you address this community problem from your position as Parish Nurse in your church? How may your members respond?

2. John Pitman, a 32-year-old farmer, has been discharged from the hospital after treatment for injuries suffered in a tractor accident. He is now a paraplegic and lives in an old farmhouse on the 160-acre farm with his pregnant wife and 2 children 3 and 6 years old. It is now August and the corn and soybean crops are growing well, but the harvester is in need of repair. John and Annie wonder what they will do now; this was their first good farming year after a drought of 3.

How would you and your Congregational Nurse program respond to this situation, given the resources you have and your ties with the community?

3. Beth Long, a Congregational Nurse in the only a church in Little River Valley and who also works as a school health nurse for the school district, has identified the symptoms of salmonella infection among some of the older adults of her congregation. On the day before, the adults met in the fellowship hall of the church with other Senior citizens of the community for the monthly SHARP Club meeting. They were served cafeteria style by 6th grade children of the community school, an inter-generational custom. The food was prepared by members of a committee; some of it was brought in from their homes, salads were made on site. Beth is working with the Public Health nurses to identify the origin of the outbreak, but at this time several of her congregational elder adults need attention.

If you were Beth, how would you use your PN leadership skills in this situation?

4. Joan Miller, Congregational Nurse, is making a home visit to a 22-year-old single new mother who has 2 other children ages 2 and 4. Joan's church has an outreach program called "Welcome Baby" and this little family was referred to her by the nurse in the hospital maternity department. The mother is in her third postpartum day; this is her first full day at home with her healthy newborn and her other children. She did not seek prenatal care for this pregnancy. She has no family locally. In fact, her relationship with her parents was reportedly dysfunctional so that they do not even know where she is. Joan worked until her delivery and had a girlfriend babysit her children. The infant's father is an occasional visitor and is sporadic in providing financial support. After establishing a helping relationship with Cindy, the mom, Joan learns of many more needs in this family: the cupboards are almost bare, the rent and utility bills are behind 2 months, the children have not seen a physician or nurse practitioner in over a year and are probably behind in their immunizations, and the apartment is inadequately furnished and dirty. *If you were Joan, what actions would you take to help this family?*

PRESENTATIONS

The following slideshows are included to reinforce learning by giving visual concepts to the content of this course.

Slide 1

Introduction

- Community: Multiple definitions

- Objective:
  - Establish a characterization of community and the types of communities that exist.
    - Broad definition of community
    - Types of communities
      - Boundaries
      - Interaction of members
      - Perceived ability to solve problems

Community has multiple definitions. The World Health Organization (WHO) has given the most common definition as "a collective body of individuals identified by geography, common interests, concerns, characteristics, or values" (Pender, Murdaugh & Parsons, 2006, p. 75). McKnight (2002) relates that community as defined, is a broad term which can and does include "an association, a self-generated gathering of common people or citizens who have the creativity and capacity to solve problems. Regardless of how community is defined, the members of a community must share a sense of values and are usually united for the common good However, there are similarities that pervade any definition of community giving a broad sense of community upon which to build a definition that is common to all. Regardless of how community is defined, the members of a community share a sense of values and are usually united for the common good.

This presentation seeks to understand the characterization of community and the types of communities that exist by establishing a broad definition of community, and defining the types of communities in relation to their boundaries, interaction of members and perceived ability to solve problems.

Slide 3

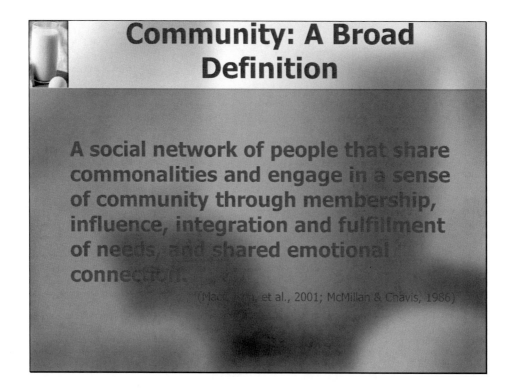

The broad definition of community does not make any distinctions between types of communities but does delineate the foundation of what constitutes a community. Communities are based upon what people have in common. Whether that commonality exists in the form of a geographic boundary, a disease process, beliefs, ethnicity, or anything that brings them together as a unit and creates interaction amongst members in the pursuit of something greater for the community rather than the individual. The characteristics of any community are born of the needs of people who share commonalities thereby creating a sense of community. The sense of community that is hallmark to all communities is that they consist of membership based upon what is common between all members creating a sense of emotional safety, belonging, identity, and personal investment (McMillan & Chavis ,1986). Influence refers to the empowerment (McMillan & Chavis, 1986) of the community and therefore the community has the ability to influence not only its members but others beyond the confines of the community. However, within the community the influence guides the rules, values, norms and conduct within the community, whether they are formal or informal. Integration and fulfillment of needs refers to the needs that are common to the community. Shared emotional connection is what forms the social ties and creates the cohesiveness of a community.

The differing types of communities can be formal or informal in nature, have boundaries that are tangible or intangible, be homogeneous or diverse, and function in a negative or positive capacity. Regardless of the type of community that exists, each can be defined by their boundaries, interaction of members, and ability to solve problems.

Slide 4

Face to Face Communities

Communities
- Seminars, classroom settings
- Church meetings

Boundaries
- Within the confines of the room

Interaction of Members
- Communication –verbal, nonverbal

Ability to Solve Problems
- Open communication

(Friedman, et al., 2003, p.24)

Community Health Nurse
- Facilitates, organizes
- Teaching, counseling
- Collaboration
- Role modeling

The face to face communities have the opportunity to interact in person thereby imparting a personal touch and tone to the interactions. Face to face communities include seminars, classroom settings, church functions, political rallies, etc… (Yihong, 2004). Members interact with each other through verbal or nonverbal forms of communication which requires a sender of a message, a form/channel of the message, a receiver, and interaction between the receiver and the sender (Friedman, Bowden, Jones, 2003). The ability to solve problems is by open communication. "Open communication involves introducing new information, correcting misinformation, problem solving, having and resolving misunderstandings and conflicts" (Friedman et al., 2003, p.5). The community health nurse can approach or use this type of community in many ways.

Slide 5

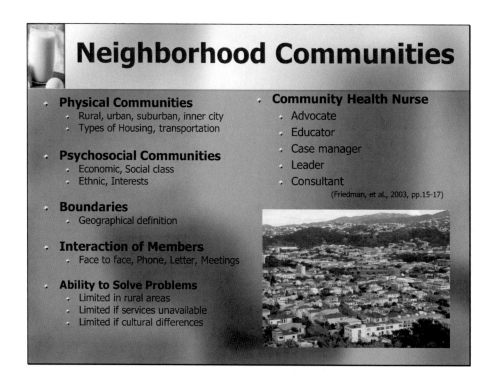

Neighborhood communities have many different characteristics. Friedman, Bowden, and Jones (2003), describe the significance of neighborhoods:
•The neighborhood and community in which the family lives exerts a tremendous influence on the health of the family.
•The neighborhood and adjoining community can be described relative to their physical and their psychosocial impact on families.
•The neighborhood and wider community that the family lives in have definite effects on family health.
•Substantial social and economic homogeneity has existed in most of the communities that have been studied (p. 254-255).

Neighborhood communities can be delineated through physical constructs such as rural, inner city, types of housing, health status, or through psychosocial constructs such as economic status, social class, ethnicity, or interests. The neighborhood communities geographically defined via roads, blocks, and areas. Interaction among these members take place in the form of face to face, telecommunications, letters, newsletters, meetings and internet. The community health nurse (CHN) can approach neighborhoods as a consultant, advocate, educator, and leader, in providing information, resources to promote health and prevent disease. The CHN can aid in the attainment of needed services such as transportation and educate and consult on the neighborhood environmental health.

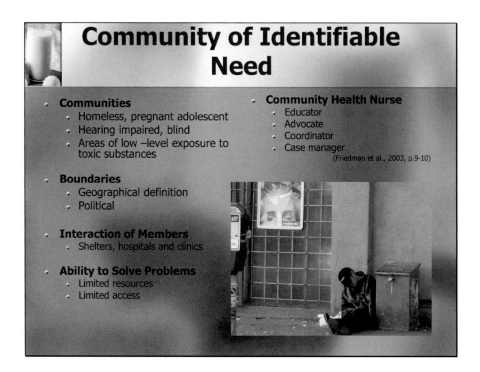

"Homelessness in cities and temperate regions, has risen sharply in the United States since 1980" (Taylor, 1995 as cited in Friedman et al., 2003, p.9). "There are interventions designed to initiate community action for improved environments related to community coping" (Friedman, Bowdon, and Jones, 2003, p. 261). Community health nurses working with homeless families stress the importance of showing respect toward these clients, being non-threatening, assuming a low profile, and minimizing reporting and paperwork. (Vernez, Burnam, McGlynn, Trude, and Mittman, 1988 as cited in Friedman, Bowdon, and Jones, 2003).

Examples of communities of identifiable need consist of the homeless community, pregnant adolescent community, hearing impaired community, areas of low-level exposure to toxic substances. The homeless community has been identified as lacking affordable housing, being poor, and that families with children are the fastest growing community of homeless in the United States with a statistic of 500,000 families (Friedman et al., 2003). Communities of low-level exposure to toxic substances would consist of areas with polluted drinking water, polluted air, contaminated food, high crime rates, and unsafe play areas. Members of communities of identifiable needs suffer chronic health problems, loneliness, depression and therefore interactions often take place within shelters, hospitals, clinics.

The CHN can approach this community as an educator, advocate, coordinator, case manager through assessment of the environment of the shelter, providing information to access health care, providing the resources to be able to access health care and other need resources, coordinate referrals and conduct safety assessments.

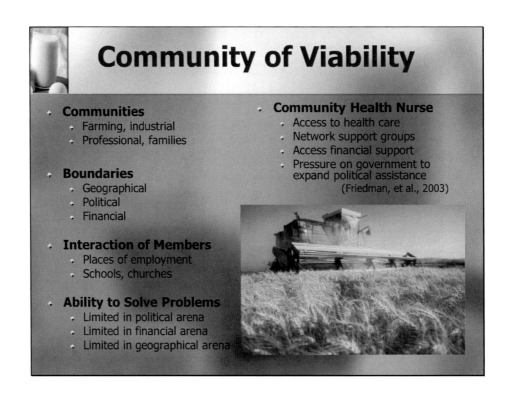

Community of Viability

Communities
- Farming, industrial
- Professional, families

Boundaries
- Geographical
- Political
- Financial

Interaction of Members
- Places of employment
- Schools, churches

Ability to Solve Problems
- Limited in political arena
- Limited in financial arena
- Limited in geographical arena

Community Health Nurse
- Access to health care
- Network support groups
- Access financial support
- Pressure on government to expand political assistance

(Friedman, et al., 2003)

"Satisfaction with neighborhoods and community has been found to be closely associated with satisfaction with life in general. The sociopolitical environment encompasses an enormous arena with complex factors interacting to create circumstances which may enable or limit communities" (Friedman, Bowdon, and Jones, 2003, p. 11). These communities are dependent upon something for viability, as in the farming communities.

Slide 8

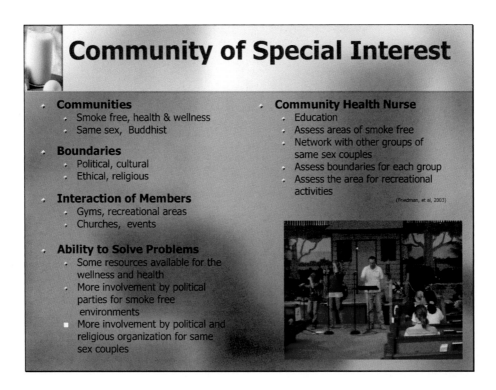

"The suprasystem (sociopolitical, economic environment) may pose the greatest challenge to resolving environmental stressors" (Friedman, et al., 2003, p.3). "Community level interventions that could affect families' community and sociopolitical environments are providing opportunities for community members to meet and discuss the situation, promote community competence in coping, and establish methods to access information and support for the targeted issue" (Carpenito, 2000, as cited in Friedman, Bowdon, and Jones, 2003, p. 17).

Slide 9

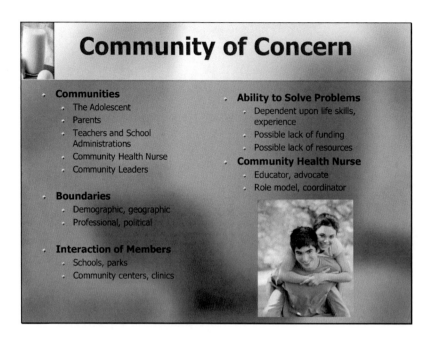

The particular community of concern to be addressed here is that of alcohol, tobacco and drug use and abuse among the youth of our communities. The old saying that "it takes a village to raise a child" is as true today as ever. Because of peer pressure, adolescents are completely vulnerable to the risks of becoming involved with these substances, and falling prey to a multitude of problems associated with them. The community health nurse, in conjunction with community resources, can educate teachers and parents to prevent children from starting down the destructive path of substance abuse. (Community of Concern, 2004).

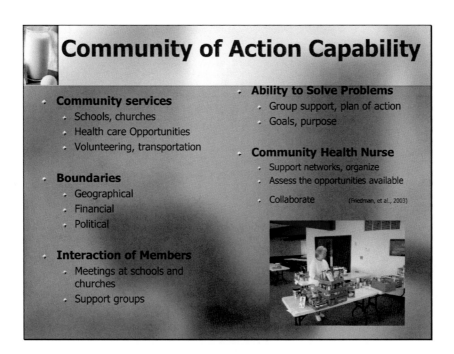

"Healthy families are those that are active and reach out in self-initiating ways to relate to various community groups"
(Lewis & Associates, 1976; McCubbin & McCubbin, 1993, as cited in Friedman et al., 2003, p. 258).

Slide 11

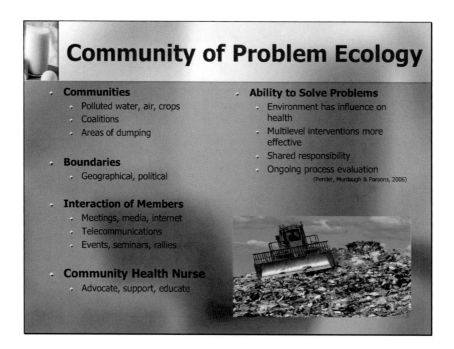

In models of social ecology, the community is considered an open system where interactions occur among its members as well as between community members and the environment. Parts of the community, according to Lowry & Martin and Schuster & Goeppinger as cited by Pender et al. (2006), are made of parts that are interrelated as well as independent, and are organized to function for the good of the community. These parts include the schools, health care systems, schools and churches, law enforcement and fire protection, economics and areas of recreation (Pender, Murdaugh, & Parsons, 2006).

The concept of community ecology relates to the relationship between these parts and community. In understanding the ecology, we understand the interaction of people with their environment, whether physical, social, or cultural. Building a healthy community must address many factors that can affect the well-being of its members. Community leaders and members need to share the responsibility for the health of the community and join forces in order to create an environment that encourages health and wellness.

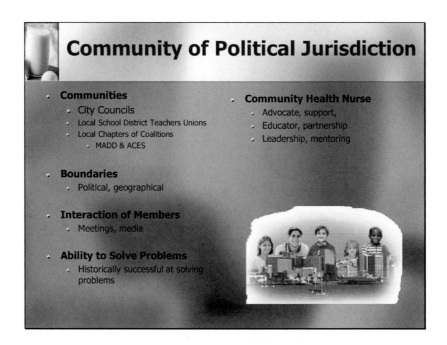

Examples of the community of political jurisdiction can include can include city council members, members of unions, such as teachers and local chapters of coalitions such as Mothers Against Drunk Drivers (MADD) and Association for Children for Enforcement of Support (ACES) who may be involved in political or legislative activity that affects the health and general welfare of the community at large.

The interaction between the members used in the example, would be through organized meetings. The interaction within the community would be in a variety of ways, the newspaper and radio, informational flyers, radio etc.

The boundaries of these communities particular communities would be geographic as the participants would be limited to individuals in certain school districts, townships, counties, for example. Historically these communities have been instrumental in solving problems within their community, therefore the perceived ability for them to do so would be present.

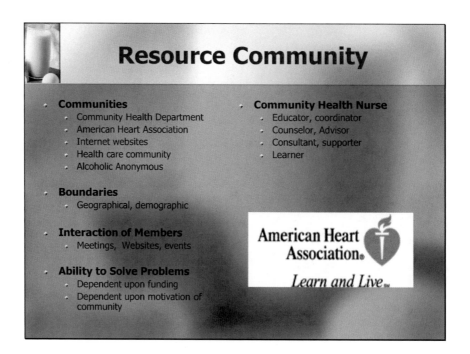

Resource communities provide requirements for the community, whether they are in the form of information, support, advocacy, or tangible needs. The boundaries for some of the Resource community would be again, geographical, and include only people within a township or county etc. The internet is a boundary free community, making information available to anyone with access.

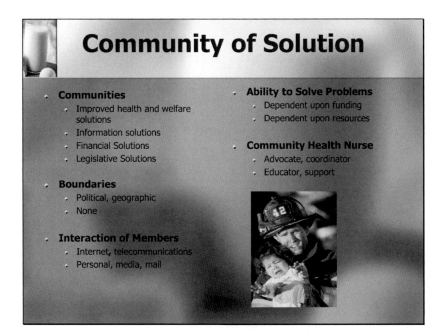

The community of solution encompasses all communities that have a purpose or a goal to accomplish. The boundaries for the solution community can be geographic, or with no limits when internet solutions are introduced. Depending on the goal of the community, these solutions can be obtained in different ways through directly improving health, providing information, finances or seeking important legislation.

Slide 15

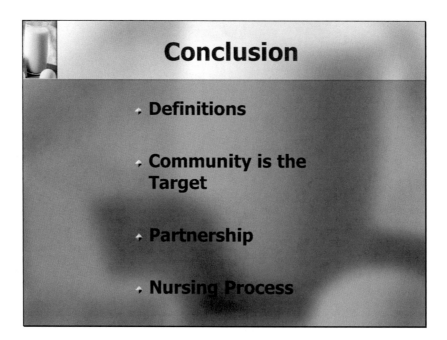

In conclusion, we have determined that there are many definitions of community. All of the definitions point to the fact that there the dimensions of community include interpersonal relationships, common locale and shared interests. The practice of community nursing is targeted to the population in which changes to improve health are desired. To improve community health, partnerships are formed between the residents and different health care disciplines. To provide appropriate community health care, the nursing process is used in a variety of ways, starting with data collection and its analysis. Priorities are established after data analysis and goals and objectives identified. Goals and objectives are met by the interventions that are identified to accomplish said goals. Evaluation occurs when the community health nurse has determined the effects of his or her work.

Slide 16

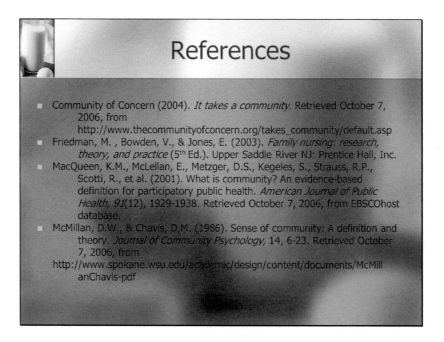

References

- Community of Concern (2004). *It takes a community.* Retrieved October 7, 2006, from
  http://www.thecommunityofconcern.org/takes_community/default.asp
- Friedman, M. , Bowden, V., & Jones, E. (2003). *Family nursing: research, theory, and practice* (5th Ed.). Upper Saddle River NJ: Prentice Hall, Inc.
- MacQueen, K.M., McLellan, E., Metzger, D.S., Kegeles, S., Strauss, R.P., Scotti, R., et al. (2001). What is community? An evidence-based definition for participatory public health. *American Journal of Public Health, 91*(12), 1929-1938. Retrieved October 7, 2006, from EBSCOhost database.
- McMillan, D.W., & Chavis, D.M. (1986). Sense of community: A definition and theory. *Journal of Community Psychology,* 14, 6-23. Retrieved October 7, 2006, from
  http://www.spokane.wsu.edu/academic/design/content/documents/McMillanChavis-pdf

Slide 17

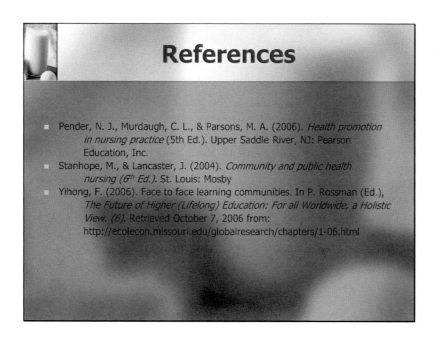

References

- Pender, N. J., Murdaugh, C. L., & Parsons, M. A. (2006). *Health promotion in nursing practice* (5th Ed.). Upper Saddle River, NJ: Pearson Education, Inc.
- Stanhope, M., & Lancaster, J. (2004). *Community and public health nursing (6th Ed.).* St. Louis: Mosby
- Yihong, F. (2006). Face to face learning communities. In P. Rossman (Ed.), *The Future of Higher (Lifelong) Education: For all Worldwide, a Holistic View. (6).* Retrieved October 7, 2006 from:
  http://ecolecon.missouri.edu/globalresearch/chapters/1-06.html

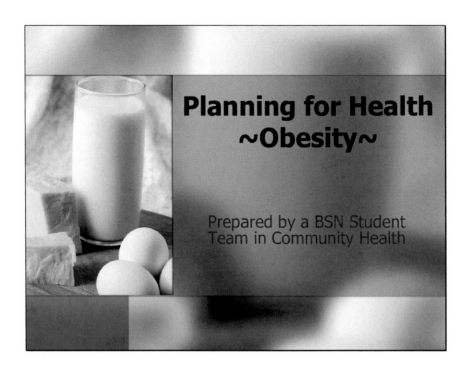

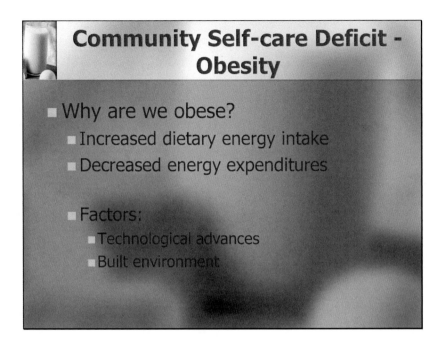

The prevalence of obesity has markedly increased in the past few decades, and this disorder is responsible for more health care expenditures than any other medical condition (Hensrud & Klein, 2006). The greater the body mass index (BMI) (Calculated as weight in kilograms divided by the square of height in meters), the greater the risk of co-morbidities, including diabetes mellitus, hypertension, obstructive sleep apnea, many cancers, dyslipidemia, cardiovascular disease, and overall mortality (Hensrud & Klein, 2006). The prevalence of extreme obesity is greater among women than among men and greater among blacks than among non-Hispanic whites or Hispanics (Hensrud & Klein, 2006). The effect of extreme obesity on mortality is greater among young than among older adults, greater among men than among women, and greater among whites than among blacks (Hensrud & Klein, 2006). The current permissive environment that promotes increased dietary energy intake and decreased energy expenditures through reduced daily physical activity coupled with genetic susceptibility is an important pathogenic factor.

Until very recently in the history of human existence, obtaining enough food for survival was a major challenge and regular physical activity was unavoidable. Technological advances and the built environment have resulted in a progressive increase in average body weight and BMI. Moreover, the prevalence of extreme obesity, has greatly increased in the United States (Hensrud & Klein, 2006).

The aggregate population addressed in this presentation are adults who are obese or overweight. The commonality of these people is poor eating habits and lack of exercise. The problem goes beyond the local communities and is an international problem spanning every nation and economic group.

The nurse works with individuals or groups within the community, but the outcomes of the nursing interventions affect the entire community beyond their immediate boundaries. "An obesity pandemic threatens to overwhelm health systems around the globe with illnesses such as diabetes and heart disease... The World Health Organization says more than 1 billion adults are overweight and 300 million of them are obese" (Rohan, 2006, ¶1, ¶3).

Dr. Phillip James, the British chairman of the International Obesity Task Force states that this is an enormous problem that is already accepted, and is going to overwhelm every medical system in the world (as cited in Rohan, 2006).

The adult community deficit of obesity is thought to be both a nurse identified and community identified problem. A community identified problem because some members of the community are aware of the obesity problem within the community and are interested in reducing the incidence of obesity. It is also a nurse identified problem because as the nurse observed and assessed the community she identified obesity as a problem, however others in the community may not recognize the problem due to lack of awareness, lack of information, cultural views and beliefs.

Obesity is affecting our lifestyle, our children, and our health. Targeting the adult population with a focus to be involved in a health promotion program that is both educative and supportive in nature will allow the community to promote health and wellness and will transition to their children through modeling of behavior.

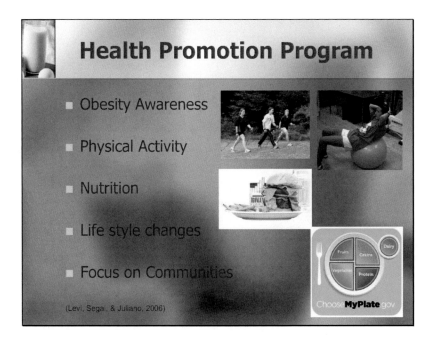

A health promotion program that concentrates on educating the community about physical activity, nutrition, and life style changes in relation to obesity was focused on because the majority of Americans do not participate in the recommended amount of physical activity. In 2003, 54.1 percent of adult Americans failed to meet the recommended guidelines for physical activity (Levi, Segal, & Juliano, 2006). A 2003 research group concluded higher physical activity and lower obesity levels could be seen in more " walkable" communities (Levi et al., 2006). Research focuses on food availability in relationship to cost and accessibility (Levi et al., 2006). Lower income people have less access and pay more for fruits and vegetables. America's eating habits have changed. Adults consume more calories, bigger portion sizes, fewer fruits, vegetables and whole grains, more sugar, more dietary fat, a drop in drinking milk and a large increase in drinking soda and fruit juice and there is a major increase in eating out (Levi et al., 2006). On the individual level, successful obesity intervention strategies incorporate dietary and physical activity changes into daily life on a permanent and ongoing basis (Levi et al., 2006). This requires a lifelong, comprehensive commitment to behavioral change. On the broader, public health level, efforts must focus on the long term(Levi et al., 2006).

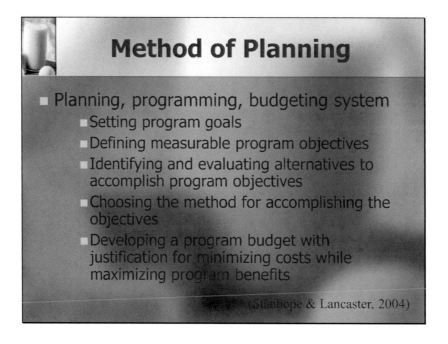

The Planning, Programming, and Budgeting System (PPBS) was chosen for this community self-care deficit. When developing a program based on the needs of a community it is important to have a structured method to set goals and evaluate programs. This is especially true when community health programs are operating with a limited budget. The model is appealing because it allows for identification and evaluation of alternatives to the program objectives. It gives flexibility where other methods of planning do not.

Because PPBS uses objectives that can be operationally defined by nursing standards or performance criteria, it is a system that lends itself to effective program evaluation (Stanhope & Lancaster, 2004, p. 506)

Slide 23

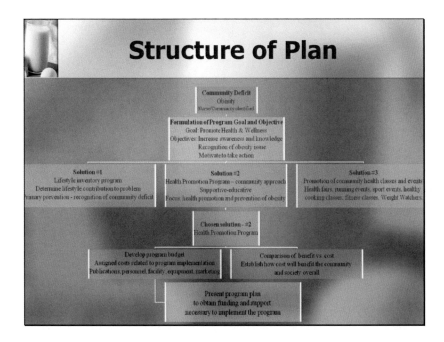

The development of the program was based upon the framework of the planning, programming, and budgeting system (PPBS) planning method. The first step in planning the project was to accurately identify the need and recognize that the need was nurse and community identified. The problem is identified in this way, as the community may not recognize obesity as a community self-care deficit. The goal and objectives were established based upon the identified community deficit and recognition that lack of awareness and information regarding obesity is contributing to the ongoing prevalence of obesity. With goals and objectives established, three solutions are developed with relevant required resources detailed for each solution. These solutions were then analyzed to determine which solution would best accomplish meeting the goal and objectives, be easily implemented and put to use by the community. This health promotion program solution was chosen because it was the program that is thought to best achieve the set objectives. The program then needed to have a budget in place with all expenses assigned. In addition, a comparison of the actual cost compared to benefit needs to be determined. If the benefit can be shown to be sustainable and equal to or greater than the cost, chances of obtaining funding for implementation of the program are increased. When all elements of the plan are in order, the plan needs to be presented to those who would be providing support and funding to the initiative. If funding is granted, more detailed work of implementing and further detailed planning and budgeting is required in order to sustain the program or to develop the program further to a more participatory phase of implementation. It is the goal of the program that the community recognizes obesity as a community problem and decides that they are ready to act in prevention and recovery of the problem. It takes a strong support system to lose weight, get fit and maintain a healthy lifestyle.

Slide 24

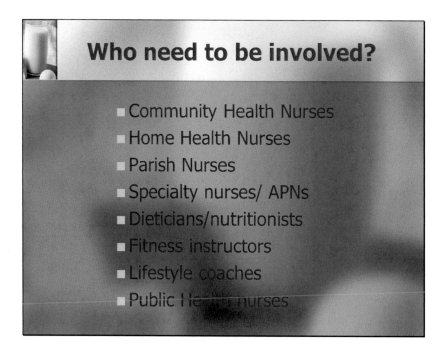

The human resources needed to make the program effective require a collaboration of differing specialties and roles. The community health nurse cannot do this on her/his own. He/she needs the help and expertise in the areas that are being focused on within the program. The community health nurse takes on many roles in this health program, from development of the program, to directing it, to obtaining funding for it, and staffing it. The home health nurses are incorporated as they enter the community and work with community members in their homes and they are great sources to initiated obesity awareness and education and to promote the program within the community. Parish nurses within the community are another source of education and awareness and can work with the community health nurse to establish a presence of health promotion amongst parish members. They can work closely together to provide what is needed for the community. Specialty nurses and advance practice nurses would be used in the capacity to deliver teaching seminars on interventions related to obesity, on the comorbidities of obesity, such as peripheral vascular disease, congestive heart failure, etc. Dieticians, nutritionists, fitness instructors, and lifestyle coaches would provide seminars and classes as available and needed. The public health nurse would be used as a resource for the ongoing program. The PHN would be used for advice and information about implementing, maintaining and funding the program.

Slide 25

The pandemic of obesity is overwhelming the United States. Obesity is non-selective, and mostly self-inflicted and people of all ages, races, and social classes are affected. The community health nurse works with individuals within his or her community, but the outcomes of teaching programs have effects that reach far outside the confines of the immediate community boundaries.

Using various planning methods, community health nurses can promote programs that teach awareness, promote lifestyle changes that include proper nutrition and physical activity which focus on all members of the community who are in need.

Slide 26

References

- Hensrud, D., & Klein, S. (2006, October) Extreme obesity: A new medical crisis in the United States. *Mayo Clinic Proceedings*. V81, pg S5. Retrieved October 19, 2006, from ProQuest Database.

- Levi, J., Segal, L.M., & Juliano, C. (2006, August). F as in fat: How obesity policies are failing in America 2006. An issue report presented at the meeting of the Obesity Coalition for Missouri, Jefferson City, Mo. Retrieved October 14, 2006, from the Trust for America's Health Web site: www.healthyamericans.org

- Rohan, S. (2006, September 4) Experts warn of deadly global pandemic at obesity meeting [Electronic version]. *Beaumont Enterprise*, p.A15. Retrieved October 14th, 2006, from ProQuest database.

- Stanhope, M., & Lancaster, J. (2004). *Community and public health nursing* (6thed.). St. Louis, MO: Mosby.

Slide 27

Slide 28

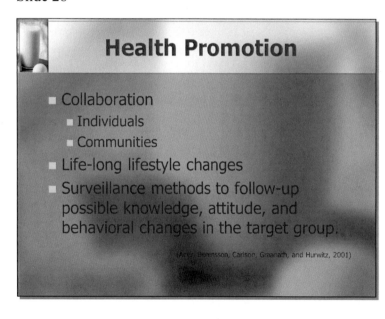

Sustained behavior changes require long–term strategies at the individual level and community level. Practitioners suggest that strategies must focus on supporting lifelong lifestyle changes and working with communities to help make it easier for people to make these changes in their lives (Levi, Segal, and Juliano, 2006).

Long term wellness depends on "individual obesity intervention strategies incorporate dietary and physical activity changes into daily life on a permanent and ongoing basis. This requires a lifelong, comprehensive commitment to behavioral change" (Levi, et al., 2006).

On the public health level, efforts must focus on the long term and this requires the political will to provide enough funding to adequately support the development, implementation, and ongoing evaluation of large-scale obesity intervention studies" (Levi, et al., 2006).

Health promotion is a community problem and nurses will assist with assessments, organizing, analyzing, implementing and evaluating the program. Commitment by the individual and community is essential for success.

Slide 29

Quality Assurance (QA) Plan

Short Term Goal: Behavioral and knowledge changes-Education

- **Awareness of Healthy Eating**
  - **Example: Eating 5 fruits or 3 vegetable a day**
  - QA- Did the participant eat 5 fruits or 3 vegetables a day?
    Yes_____ No_____

- **Increase in physical activity to 30 minutes 4xs a week**
  - QA – Did the participant exercise four times a week for 30 minutes.
    Yes_____ No _____

  - QA – Did the participant participate in any health changing classes this month?
    Yes_____ No _____

(Shape Up Missouri, 2006)

An article in Health Promotion International states "Quality assurance studies show that health promotion work can be both human-welfare promoting and a cost–effective way of handling health problems... Quality assurance differs from evaluation in that it focuses ongoing work rather any final outcome at a given point in time" (Ader, Berensson, Carlsson, Granath, & Urwitz, 2001, ¶3,¶5).

Quality Assurance will focus on the ongoing process of health promotion. There are so many different aspects of health that it is an ongoing process. "Quality assurance is often described as a continuous and dynamic process" (Neuhauser as cited in Ader et al., 2001, ¶5).

The target population was identified as the overweight and the obese. It is important to have participation by the target group, decision- makers, and health care providers so each has the opportunity to have impact and take part in the program.

The target population must make a voluntary commitment to the program in order for the program to be successful. "Behavioral changes measure change in the target group's knowledge, attitudes and behavior" (Ader, et al., 2001, ¶32).

Slide 30

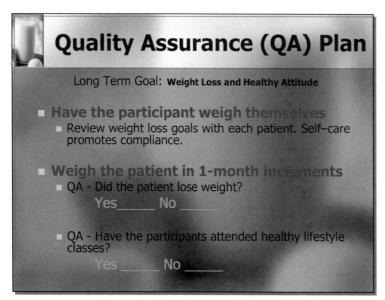

"Primary prevention is long-term by nature" (Ader et al., 2001, ¶12). "One of the most important tasks in health promotion is to reduce health inequalities between different groups in society. For this reason, it is important to consider aspects of equality in the course of goal formulation (Ader et al., 2001, ¶13).

"The outcome of a population-oriented preventive programme should be measurable in changes in epidemiological variables, i.e. changes in morbidity and mortality" (Ader et al., 2001, ¶30). Health promotions often only achieve tangible results after a long period of time. "Effects on and changes in health in a population are frequently the result of the impacts of a variety of factors. It is important to take measurements both before and after the implementation of the programme/the intervention (Ader et al., 2001, ¶31).

Slide 31

The core of any community program is the collaboration of the community, its resources and support. As shown in this illustration, when all of these factors are in place the program will run "like a well-oiled machine". However if one fails, the entire process fails. A strong commitment is required from each participant.

This community partnership model gives us a detailed view of the collaborative relationships of the health promotion program.

The goal of the program is to **educate** the community so that there is an **awareness** that obesity is a problem that can be managed and through **motivation** there will be active participation in the **promotion** of their health and well-being.

In the center is the community, the **core** of the program, the target population of adults. Working very closely with the community is the community health nurse, who will assess, organize, analyze, implement and evaluate the needs of the community. However, this requires collaboration with many others in the community.

The middle ring within the model represents the **resources**. These resources may not be involved in the actual planning of the health promotion program, but are key players in making the program successful. The public health nurse, parish nurse, dietician/nutritionist, fitness instructor, home health nurse and lifestyle coach have been identified for this health promotion program as resources and are all essential members in the implementation. However, they may serve as collaborators in identifying some of the needs of the community in their area of expertise and would be instrumental in the development of interventions that may help to meet those needs.

The **support** of the program is identified in different ways. There is physical support for the program, through volunteerism. Financial support provided by community businesses and organizations as well as legislative support, state funding, federal funding. It is through continual support both physically and financially that the program has a greater chance of success and sustainability.

This model gives structure to the program and emphasizes what is necessary to reach the goal of better health for the obese adult community.

EDUCATION, AWARNESS, MOTIVATION, AND PARTICIPATION.

Slide 33

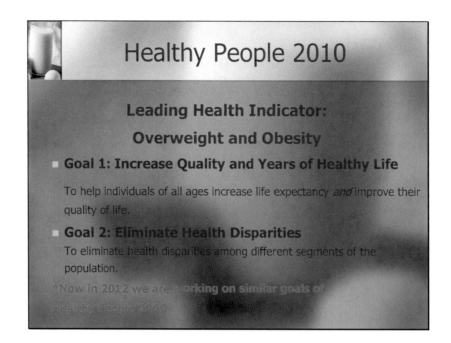

Goal One:

Healthy People 2010 sought to increase life expectancy and quality of life by helping individuals gain the knowledge, motivation, and opportunities they need to make informed decisions about their health. At the same time, Healthy People 2010 encouraged local and State leaders to develop communitywide [sic] and statewide efforts that promote healthy behaviors, create healthy environments, and increase access to high-quality health care. Given the fact that individual and community health are often inseparable, it is critical that both the individual and the community do their parts to increase life expectancy and improve quality of life (Healthy People 2010).

Goal Two:

Healthy People 2010 recognized that communities, States, and national organizations will need to take a multidisciplinary approach to achieve health equity--an approach that involves improving health, education, housing, labor, justice, transportation, agriculture, and the environment, as well as data collection itself. However, the greatest opportunities for reducing health disparities are in promoting communitywide [sic] safety, education, and access to health care, and in empowering individuals to make informed health care decisions. Healthy People 2010 is firmly dedicated to the principle that--regardless of age, gender, race or ethnicity, income, education, geographic location, disability, or sexual orientation--every person in every community across the Nation deserves equal access to comprehensive, culturally competent, community-based health care systems that are committed to serving the needs of the individual and promoting community health (Healthy People 2010).

What is a health disparity? Healthy People 2010 defined it as: an inequality or gap that exists between two or more groups. Health disparities are believed to be the result of the complex interaction of personal, societal, environmental factors (2000). It is through those complex interactions, and the steps outlined in this presentation that the CHN is well-equipped to face the challenge set forth by Healthy People 2010 and 2020 to eliminate disparities in health care, thus promoting healthier weight and good nutrition among the residents of the community.

Slide 34

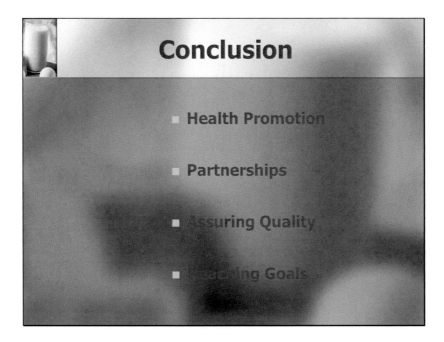

The CHN's focus on health promotion involves the collaboration of both individuals and the community in order to attain life-long lifestyle changes which result in lower weight and better overall health of all concerned. All levels of prevention are involved in this dynamic process, and community collaboration is at the core of assuring its' success. When efforts are combined to attain the goals set forth for the community, health disparities may well be eliminated, and the result will be a slimmer, well nourished, healthier community.

I thank you for your kind attention.

Slide 35

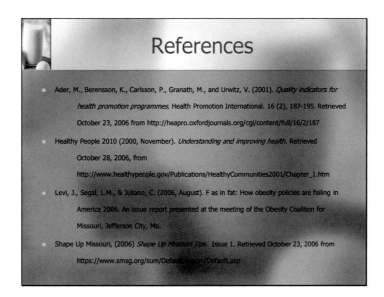

Ader, M., Berensson, K., Carlsson, P., Granath, M., and Urwitz, V. (2001). *Quality indicators for health promotion programmes*. Health Promotion International. 16 (2), 187-195. Retrieved October 23, 2006 from http://heapro.oxfordjournals.org/cgi/content/full/16/2/187

Healthy People 2010 (2000, November). *Understanding and improving health*. Retrieved October 28, 2006, from http://www.healthypeople.gov/Publications/HealthyCommunities2001/Chapter_1.htm

Levi, J., Segal, L.M., & Juliano, C. (2006, August). F as in fat: How obesity policies are failing in America 2006. An issue report presented at the meeting of the Obesity Coalition for Missouri, Jefferson City, Mo.

Shape Up Missouri, (2006) *Shape Up Missouri Tips*. Issue 1. Retrieved October 23, 2006 from https://www.smsg.org/sum/Default.asp

Congregational Nursing

Groundwork for Developing Your
Parish Nursing Practice

Tools of Our Mission

- Spiritual gifts:
- The Therapeutic Relationship in the Context of the Nursing Process
- Volunteers
- Tools for practice

Self-Inventory

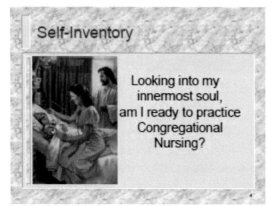

Looking into my innermost soul, am I ready to practice Congregational Nursing?

Assets

- A high level of self-awareness
- In touch with one's values
- Acting on one's values
- Prizing: cherishing and publicly affirming others
- Choosing: after consideration of consequences, freely
- Acting: with a pattern, consistency and repetition

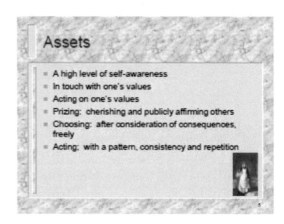

Caring (or Love)
The foundation of the helping relationship

- A response to others in a manner that expresses awareness and respect for a person as an individual, with knowledge and consideration for his specific needs and eventually mutual sharing with him.
- Unconditional acceptance of the person as he is, together with a vision of what he is capable of becoming

Empathy

The Empathy Process
- Identification - lose consciousness of self and become engrossed in the personality and situation of another
- Incorporation

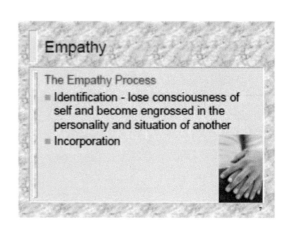

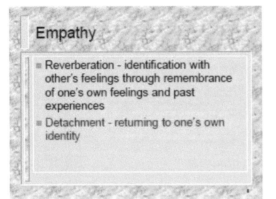

Empathy

- Reverberation - identification with other's feelings through remembrance of one's own feelings and past experiences
- Detachment - returning to one's own identity

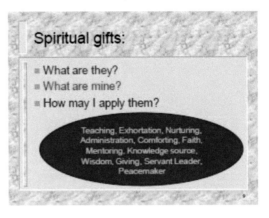

Spiritual gifts:

- What are they?
- What are mine?
- How may I apply them?

Teaching, Exhortation, Nurturing, Administration, Comforting, Faith, Mentoring, Knowledge source, Wisdom, Giving, Servant Leader, Peacemaker

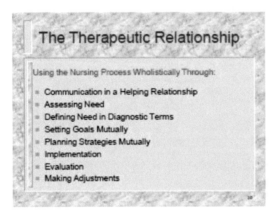

The Therapeutic Relationship

Using the Nursing Process Wholistically Through:

- Communication in a Helping Relationship
- Assessing Need
- Defining Need in Diagnostic Terms
- Setting Goals Mutually
- Planning Strategies Mutually
- Implementation
- Evaluation
- Making Adjustments

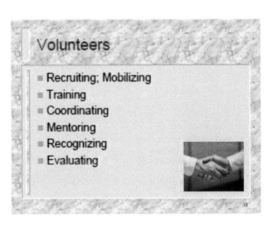

Volunteers

- Recruiting; Mobilizing
- Training
- Coordinating
- Mentoring
- Recognizing
- Evaluating

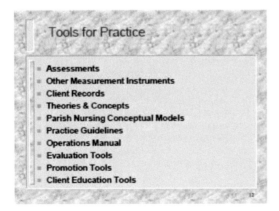

Tools for Practice

- Assessments
- Other Measurement Instruments
- Client Records
- Theories & Concepts
- Parish Nursing Conceptual Models
- Practice Guidelines
- Operations Manual
- Evaluation Tools
- Promotion Tools
- Client Education Tools

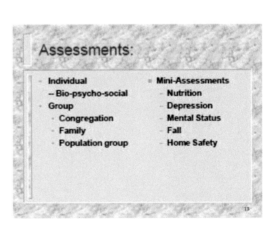

Assessments:

- Individual
  - -- Bio-psycho-social
- Group
  - Congregation
  - Family
  - Population group
- Mini-Assessments
  - Nutrition
  - Depression
  - Mental Status
  - Fall
  - Home Safety

119

Other Measurement Instruments

- Quality of Life Index
- High-level Wellness
- Spiritual Assessment
- Family Well-Being Assessment
- Social Support Scales
- Caring Scales
- Caregiver Stress/Need Scales
- Self-Care Scale (ADL,IADL)

Client Records

- Intake
- Assessments
- Nursing Intervention
- Progress Record
- Consents
- Referrals
- Volunteer Coordination
- Budget
- Evaluation

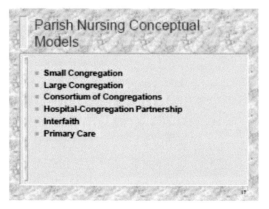

Theories & Concepts

- Caring Theory
- Multicultural
- Self-Care
- Health Belief
- Health Promotion
- Group Process
- Case Management
- Community Development

Parish Nursing Conceptual Models

- Small Congregation
- Large Congregation
- Consortium of Congregations
- Hospital-Congregation Partnership
- Interfaith
- Primary Care

Practice Guidelines

- Of the American Nurses Association-Health Ministries Association
- Of Denomination
- Of Church
- Of Parish Nurse

Operations Manual

- Mission, Purpose
- Goals
- Objectives
- Organization
- Function
- Leadership
- Job Description
- Description of Programs & Services
- Protocol of PN Service

Evaluation Tools

- Client Progress Records
- Re-Assessments
- Surveys
- Formative & Summative Reports
- Performance Review
- Outcomes
- Interviews (clients, clergy, etc.)

Promotion Tools

- Media announcements, ads, articles
- Radio, TV programs, Interviews
- Brochures, Fliers
- Newsletters
- Co-Sponsoring events
- Screening events
- Entertainment events
- Presentations, lectures, workshops

Client Education Tools

- Newsletters
- Fact Sheets
- Videos, audio tapes
- Computer programs
- Internet BBS, web page
- Presentation by slide, poster

Ethical/Legal Concerns

Ethical
- The Nurse Practice Act
- Standards of Care
- Rights of the Client
- Informed consent
- Agreement/contract with pastor

Legal
- Licensure
- Liability

Informed Consent

- Adequate information about the intervention/relationship
- Knows risk vs. benefit
- Assuming that client is capable of comprehending the info
- Has the power of free choice
- Voluntary
- Reserving the right to change his mind

Visiting Guidelines
(Therapeutic Communication)

1. Listen without interruption
2. Avoid defensiveness
3. Use a "sad but glad" statement
4. Express empathy
5. Ask questions to understand the problem
6. Find out what is expected of you
7. Explain what you can & cannot do
8. Fully discuss alternatives
9. Take action
10. F/U to ensure satisfaction

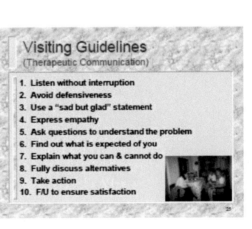

Assessing for Spiritual Well-Being

Based on 3 Factors:
1. faith/belief dimension
2. life/self-responsibility
3. life satisfaction/self-actualization

Spiritual Distress

An experience of profound disharmony in the client's belief or value system that threatens the meaning of the client's life.

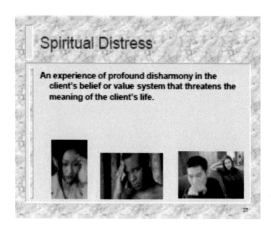

Parish Nursing as a Function of Community Health

- While assessing individuals, considers the family, the church, the community
- Promotes health
- Coordinates care through collaboration with agencies
- Monitors wellness state of congregants
- Advocates for access to health care
- Demonstrates cultural competency

Case Management of Vulnerable Populations

Reference Article
Jacquelyn Flaskerud & Betty Winslow of UCLA School of Nursing
"Conceptualizing Vulnerable Populations
Health-Related Research"
Nursing Research.
March/April, 1998, pp 69-78.

Defining Vulnerable Populations

- Social groups who experience limited resources and consequent high relative risk for morbidity and premature mortality with diminished quality of life

Fundamental Causes of Increased Susceptibility to Disease

- Low social and economic status
- Lack of environmental resources

Who Are Vulnerable?

- the poor
- those subjected to discrimination, intolerance, subordination and stigma
- those politically marginalized, disenfranchised, and denied human rights

Who Are They Really?

- women
- children
- ethnic people of color
- immigrants
- gays
- homeless
- elderly

What are the Resources?

- Human Capital operational terms:
  - income
  - jobs
  - education
  - housing

Resources . . .

- Social Connectedness/Integration
  - Marginalized, discriminated against, and stigmatized people are not
  - Inequality in role relationships (jobs, agencies)
  - Female-headed households
    - less connection
    - less economic resources
    - decreased access to community resources
  - Elderly; Those living alone

Resources . . .

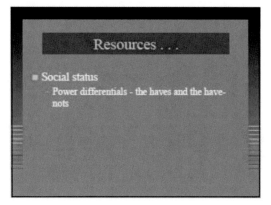

- Social status
  - Power differentials - the haves and the have-nots

Environmental Resources

Operational terms:
- access to health care
- quality of care

Centers around:
1. unserved and underserved areas
2. insurance coverage
3. service delivery environments (HMO vs. FFS)

Examples

- Children with chronic disease
- Disabled youth and young adults
- Elderly with chronic disease
- Homeless and runaway teen females
- Homeless women with substance abuse
- Mentally ill/Mentally retarded

Scenario of a Rural Community Dweller

- 65 y.o. female w/ MS, lives alone in cabin in mountains, 15 miles from town, no transp
- 50 scattered homes & farms

Assure access to health care, quality of life, and hold down cost

Scenario of an Urban Community Dweller

- A 30 yr. old male with paraplegia and cognitive and physical consequences of hydrocephalus, in minimally-assisted living congregate home supported by federal entitlement funding. Parents, 65+ years old, are physically unable to care for him.

Scenario of a Marginalized Community Dweller

- A 25 year-old Central American pregnant provisionally documented immigrant, working as a personal housekeeper, recently escaped from bondage to a pimp, and seeking access to citizenship for health care, education assistance, and community connections.

. . . And so the stories go on. The opportunities of service are numerous. Are you up to it?

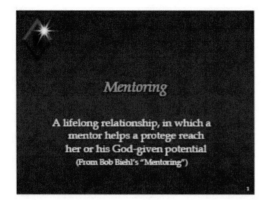

Mentoring

A lifelong relationship, in which a
mentor helps a protege reach
her or his God-given potential
(From Bob Biehl's "Mentoring")

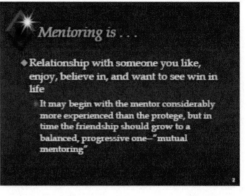

Mentoring is . . .

- Relationship with someone you like,
  enjoy, believe in, and want to see win in
  life
  - It may begin with the mentor considerably
    more experienced than the protege, but in
    time the friendship should grow to a
    balanced, progressive one—"mutual
    mentoring"

Mentoring . . .

- Intentionalizes a relationship
  - Beyond the friendship, there is an accepted
    motive—the mentor is available to the
    protege, even in the middle of the night.
- Asks questions like:
  - What are your priorities?
  - How can I help you?

Mentoring is Making Progress

- In family and marriage
- Financially
- In personal growth
- Physically
- Professionally
- Socially
- Spiritually

*The Mentoring Relationship is
Formed When You Say:*

"I love you, I believe in you, I
want to help you succeed. I
want to make my resources and
experience available to you to
help you become all that God
wants you to be."

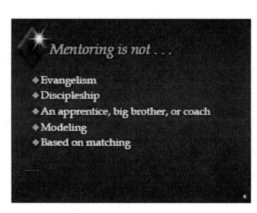

Mentoring is not . . .

- Evangelism
- Discipleship
- An apprentice, big brother, or coach
- Modeling
- Based on matching

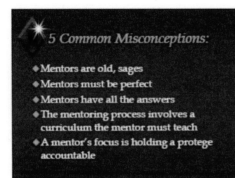

5 Common Misconceptions:

- Mentors are old, sages
- Mentors must be perfect
- Mentors have all the answers
- The mentoring process involves a curriculum the mentor must teach
- A mentor's focus is holding a protege accountable

Mentoring in a professional setting gives the protege a major advantage, a tremendous head start, because it moves the protege from the trial and error process of growing professionally to a track record simulating the mentor. The wisdom is at hand to make better-informed decisions—all those things that are not in the manuals.

Mentoring provides . . .

- Security on the Mountain of Life
  - Someone is there during trials & disappointments with a goal of seeing you through it successfully
- A bridge to the young that allows maturity into adulthood

"Let us hold fast the confession of our hope without wavering, for He who promised is faithful.

And let us consider how to stimulate one another to love and good deeds,

Not forsaking our own assembling together. . . encouraging one another, and all the more, as you see the day drawing near."

Hebrews 10:23-25

Empowering the Congregational Nurse

Congregational Nursing & Lay Health Promoter Services

Volume 2

Operations Manual

A non-profit faith consortium health ministry of

Connections of Hope
123 Sunrise Drive
Anytown, U.S.A.

Developed by Linda Royer, PhD, RN
FrameWork Health, Inc.
2012, 2019

Empowering the Congregational Nurse

Table of Contents

INTRODUCTION

(Using an imagined organization start-up plan)

The Connections of Hope is a professional, non-profit organization responding to the medical and social needs of a rural population demonstrating vulnerable status in many ways. Its mission is to create a supportive net among community stakeholders and neighboring communities by means of interfaith connections. Its significance lies in the provision of staff to congregations without nurses, linkage of congregants and their neighbors in need of community resources, and promotion of health through education, counseling, and role modeling.

Connections of Hope has three objectives:
> (1) Increase access to, and participation in, health education programming to isolated or disenfranchised residents of the Pine Tree Valley,
> (2) To expand use of community health and human service resources,
> (3) To provide professional and organizational support to formal and informal nursing activities in spiritual communities.

Columbia County and neighboring counties are recognizing the benefits of such a ministry and are requesting it. As this regional population grows, needs increase that reflect metropolitan profiles. Needs become more complex; health care services must expand and increase in methodology. Thus the need to establish Connections of Hope (COH) which will promote nursing services to spiritual communities composed of churches, synagogues, mosques and meeting places through:

- identification of congregants' health-related needs
- matching the identified needs with available resources within and among spiritual communities
- increasing the bond within the spiritual community
- promoting health through programming and services in the context of faith
- reaching beyond the spiritual communities with programming and services through prepared congregants and their authorized nurses
- providing professional support and training of nurses within their congregations
- Providing training of lay health advisors to assist congregational nurses

Purpose of Connections of Hope

Two hundred churches as small as 17 members and as large as 1200 serve Anytown and Columbia County. Interest in learning about the benefits of congregational nursing is growing among some churches. Nurses and pastors in congregations are asking for help in addressing the needs of their members. A survey among the pastors of these congregations conducted Fall, 2018, revealed that, of 70 respondents, 53% registered an interest in learning more about congregational nursing and Connections of Hope through a presentation, 34% have more health-related requests than they can handle, 64% have other health professionals in their churches, but only 13% have a health ministry.

Physicians express the desire to refer patients to a practicing health professional who can discuss and explore concepts that bring peace of mind and heart and discipline of the body into the healing process. Congregational nurses have a unique opportunity to autonomously implement targeted, appropriate, population-based wellness interventions with measurable outcomes by applying community health nursing methods.

To respond to these expressed needs Connections of Hope is developing health care delivery that trains and coordinates congregational nurses in their own settings, seeks to provide staff to churches without nurses in the membership, links congregational members and their neighbors in need with community resources, and promotes wholistic health through education, counseling, and role modeling. Connections of Hope will function as a ministry directed by interfaith needs rather than as an institution driven by marketing concerns and profitability.

Mission:

> **To create a net of wholistic professional and lay support within and between spiritual communities, and by extension to the community at large, through the connection of people in need with people who respond to God's call to service and love.**

Wisconsin, Illinois, and Pennsylvania are example states in which Congregational Nursing has demonstrated cost effective and satisfying methods of nursing care beyond the walls of institutional case management. It has also served to increase and strengthen membership of churches. An interfaith approach gives structure to existent activities, economizes effort, and supports Public Health ideals of optimizing services through collaborative partnerships. Connections of Hope incorporates those same ideals.

Conceptual Framework for Service

Philosophy: The philosophy of **Connections of Hope** embraces the following concepts . . .

- We believe in the fundamental unity of human life in its physical, emotional, intellectual, social and spiritual components
- We believe in operating as a health ministry to spiritual communities
- We believe in disease prevention and early detection, health promotion, and facilitation of selfcare
- We believe that **Connections of Hope** should have a formal and identifiable structure within the local community and linkage with local health care providers and community agencies
- We believe that **Connections of Hope** witnesses to the integration of faith and healing within the community, the church, and health care settings
- We believe the church interacts with people throughout one's life and becomes especially important at times of positive or negative change, transition, illness and crisis
- We believe the church has a responsibility for the promotion and concern and care for the health of its people.

Note: the terms "church" and "spiritual communities" include all places of worship and spiritual haven.

History
[The following is an imagined biosketch]

Connections of Hope was developed from a desire of Melody Firestone, RN, MSN to respond to needs of rural communities that lack resources for health promotion and disease prevention in PineTree Valley. She believes that harmonious relationships among and between spiritual communities can emerge and grow through interventions of health that are enclosed in messages of faith; that individuals can be reached and lives changed that are otherwise unreached by traditional health care delivery efforts.

After completion of a Community Health Master's program (University of Virginia) and as a result of involvement with a broad community assessment process in Columbia County, her dream was supported and encouraged by a network of interested individuals and agencies. A Board of Directors was chosen in January 2017. Area nurses were invited to attend an evening promotion event, and funding sources for start-up support were approached. Promotion of this concept to spiritual communities and their leaders and health professionals is a continual process. A strategic plan was developed by the founder and the newly-hired staff comprised of an administrative assistant and a nurse with community health experience. In time there would be 3 certified Community Health Workers and a cadre of trained volunteers.

What is Your Story? . . .

CHAPTER ONE

STRUCTURE OF CONNECTIONS OF HOPE

I. *Organizational Roles*
   A. The Board of Directors
      The Board of Directors of **Connections of Hope** is composed of 15 individuals from the community who represent nursing of the following practice areas:
      1. Community health
      2. Management
      3. Client education and discharge planning - case management
      4. Occupational health
      5. Advance practice
      Other Board members represent business, faith, social services, community leadership, communications, marketing and fund raising.
      The COH Board assists in the development of structure and function as well as facilitates the raising of funds and management of fiscal concerns. The overriding concern is viability and sustainability of **Connections of Hope**

B. *Advisory Council*

The Advisory Council, composed of at least 15-20 members from faith and health communities, serves as a guiding force in development of service.
   C. Administrator
   The Administrator brings education and experience in community health and health
      education as well as organizational and computer skills. Development of programming and
services, structure and function, recruiting of nurses and lay individuals, promotion of COH to
spiritual communities, and communication with media and community agencies,   and
direction of volunteers comprise the responsibilities of the Administrator.
      Specific activities required to establish **Connections of Hope** are:
- write, develop, and establish health promotion programming;
- develop curriculum for training of nurses and volunteer congregational members;
- create community-based service learning experience for college students
- build community partnerships for mutual referral
- "market" to spiritual communities for participation in COH activities
- seek credentialing from emerging professional state agency
- develop a system for measuring outcomes to this unique intervention
- actively seek funding from local and distant resources
- develop a church-based perpetual funding plan.
   D. Office Assistant/Secretary

The Office Assistant/Secretary maintains telecommunications with the Administrator and other congregational nurses, maintains documentation of services and a database of volunteers and contacts, performs other secretarial duties, manages fiscal resources.

II. *Service Roles - the Congregational Nurse*

Within the past century, renewed interest in the role of spiritual communities in health care has emerged. Treating the "whole person" is becoming the paradigm of thought and service and a groundswell of belief and action is occurring in America's churches wherein wholeness is defined as human physical, mental-emotion, intellectual, social, and spiritual balance and fulfillment.

With health care delivery changes in the spirit of cutting cost and making services efficient and measurable, individuals and families are finding early release from acute care brings circumstances that may or may not be covered by insurance nor affordable. Self-care is not only becoming a mandate wherever possible, it is a necessity. The church is the one social institution uniquely structured to affect knowledge, faith, and physical dimensions of human behavior. More than 60 percent of this nation's citizens belong to a faith community, and more than 40 percent attend worship service at least once a week. The local congregation is the fastest growing social institution in the not-for-profit sector--serving all population groups of society. Many people have inadequate insurance or do not have it at all and costs continue to rise. One solution is to call people to an active role in the management of their own health and the adoption of healthy lifeways that prevent disease.

In the spiritual community, the nurse is prepared to assist congregants in this effort. He/she may take on the role as a "Minister of Health" or "Congregational Nurse." The former may emphasize health in the context of pastoral care; the latter may signify the practice of nursing in a faith context. Functions of the congregational nurse in either position requires clear expectations of role. Is the nurse considered a spiritual-health leader in the congregation and does he/she have "pastoral prerogative" to initiate visits and interventions as part of the outreach ministry of the congregation?

Whichever descriptive title is used or role understand, the nurse is not to be seen as a primary "hands on" health care giver, but one who facilitates the use of available resources of the church and the community. Critical to the understanding of all parties is that the Congregational Nurse is seen as one who does not duplicate other nursing or medical services that are available, but seeks to creatively bridge the gaps in health education and care delivery systems.

Specific activities of the Congregational Nurse include:
- Assessment of biopsychosocial and spiritual needs of faith group members and staff
- Assessment of perceived strengths and weaknesses of the faith community
- Assessment of existence and needs of those in the marginal community of faith group
- Assessment of families with perceived or observed needs
- Assessment of access to health care problems and special mobility needs

- Case Management of individuals/families with identified needs subject to referral and/or education and monitoring of support
- Introduction of and building of support systems among the members, utilizing community agencies as available, such as A.A. groups, smoking cessation, parenting, elder care/caregiving, and self-care groups
- Recruit, train, or maintain other health professionals and lay volunteers to extend services within and without the faith group
- Enrich ministerial/pastoral team's personal and corporate roles through collaboration and knowledge-building of matters related to health and self-care.

III. ***Models of Congregational Nursing-Spiritual Community Relationships***
   A. Five Models of Congregational Nursing
      1. Congregation/Paid Model
         a. Employed by congregation either full-time or part-time or paid a stipend yearly
         b. May include benefits
         c. May include supervision and/or support from Pastor or congregation
         d. May participate in external network with other congregational nurses
         e. May have malpractice coverage paid by the congregation
      2. Congregation/Volunteer Model
         a. Functions as a volunteer at specific agreed-upon hours
         b. Receives no benefits
         c. May receive supervision from pastoral staff or congregation
         d. May be a resource through participation in an external network of congregational nurses in the area
         e. May have malpractice coverage coverage paid for by the church
      3. Hospital/Agency/Paid Model
         a. Contract between congregation and institution
         b. Paid and employed by: hospital, agency such as home health
         c. Consults and assists churches or communities
         d. May participate in an external network with other congregational nurses
      4. Hospital/Agency/Volunteer Model
         a. Volunteers specific hours
         b. Has relationship with institution such as hospital, agency, etc.
         c. May have contract as well as stipend to the nurse or church
         d. Institution may provide services such as continuing education and supervision for Congregational Nurse
         e. May participate in an external network with other congregational nurses
      5. Congregational Consortium/Paid Model
         a. Contract between COH-Congregational Nurse-group of churches for   service
         b. Paid by the Consortium of Churches; receives benefits
         c. May work full- or part-time
         d. Consults with consortium pastoral team and COH Administrator
         e. Assists congregants of only consortium churches

f. May participate in an external network with other congregational nurses
6. Faith-based Primary Care Nurse-Clergy

This is an emerging role in which the critical components of this practice may include gaining the services of a nurse practitioner and nurse case manager, establishing a physician liaison, assessing congregational health care needs, providing for both primary health and continuity of care needs of congregants and those from the community the congregation serves, and maintaining the spiritual component of the faith community. The advance practice nurse with prescriptive authority can provide primary care and case management beyond the health promotion, health screening, and support programs in communities with high risk, economically deprived, and vulnerable populations. These services may be the only opportunity for undocumented or insurance-poor individuals and their children to receive health.

NOTE: In all cases, the nurse and church leadership follow steps in initiating a **Connections of Hope** contract and develop an accountability and evaluation system for the ministry.

IV. *Defining the Role of the Congregational Nurse as a Coordinator*
The Congregational Nurse works with the pastoral team and the Health Ministry Committee or body to foster the health and wellness of the members of the congregation. It is essential to the success of this health ministry that committee members, pastor(s), and nurse work compatibly together, sharing information and making referrals and planning health activities. Some of the main responsibilities of the congregational nurse in this relationship are:

A. Collaborate with the Health Ministry Committee (or the same by any other name) and the pastor(s) to develop and plan the health ministry within the congregation.

B. Meet regularly with the pastor(s) to report on the activities of the health ministry and to share information about the needs in the congregation.

C. Serve as personal health counselor

D. With the Health Ministry Committee members, plan and teach classes, secure guest speakers, coordinate support groups and special sessions on specific health topics.

E. Provide regularly screening for disease and monitoring activities; include nearby residents in the community not of the congregation; collaborate with nearby churches

F. Serve as a liaison between congregants and community resources

G. Foster a spirit of outreach to those not of the congregation

H. Maintain appropriate health ministry records (See Appendix)

I. With the help of the Health Ministry Committee and others, recruit and train volunteers to help with health ministry activities

J. Maintain contact with peers and Connections of Hope Nursing Services, Inc.

CHAPTER TWO

PROGRAMMING AND SERVICES

I. *Roles and Services of the Congregational Nurse*

As the congregational Nurse functions in her varied roles of health educator, counselor, referral agent, advocate, facilitator, and role model, she makes assessments regarding the acute and chronic health-related needs of the congregants as well as the degree to which health promotion and disease prevention is practiced by members. She determines the need for and appropriateness of programs of education and intervention. They may be of the following topics, for which resources exist either in the community or with **Connections of Hope**:

A. New Baby visitation service called "Welcome, Baby"
B. Safety in the home; reducing lifestyle risks
C. Building effective, helping relationships within the family/in the home
D. Single parent support
E. Lifestyle changes such as tobacco cessation, weight control, relaxation
F. Self-care across the life span
G. Emergency & Disaster Training
H. Health screening
I. Mobility and the Aging concerns
J. Caregiving and caregiver support
K. Senior companion networking
L. Walking program
M. Decision making
N. Money management

II. *Tools Available to the Congregational Nurse for Community Connections*

- Community-as-Partner Model
- Community-Oriented Primary Care Model
- Case Management Model
- Program Planning and Evaluation Models
- Action Research
- Social Support Group Therapy Concepts
- Healthy People 2020 Risk Indicators and Health Promotion Objectives

C. **Assessment Tools for the Congregational Nurse**

(Several of these have copyright restrictions. They can be found in searching health promotion literature.)

1. Wholistic Assessment of Spiritual Communities
2. Elder Assessments
3. Nutritional Assessments
4. Neuman Systems Model to guide Family Health Promotion
5. Family Stressor-Strength Inventory

6. Family Health Protective Behaviors Assessment
7. Profile of Moods States
8. Depression Scale
9. Well-Being Scales
10. Addiction Scale
11. Home Safety Assessment
12. Mobility Assessment
13. Social Support Assessment
14. Individual Spiritual Assessment (Royer) – See Appendices.
15. And many others . . .

CHAPTER THREE

HUMAN RESOURCE MANAGEMENT

The organization of **Connections of Hope** *is adherent to standards of the American Nurses Association, the (State) Nurse Practice Act and Board of Nursing, and faith regulatory bodies. Supportive to this is the guidance found in Holy Scriptures in Isaiah 58, which describes restorative activities of a spiritually-healthy community.*

I.   *Recruitment of Congregational Nurses*

The initial effort to identify Congregational Nurses in and out of the spiritual communities has been an invitation to the Opening Reception of **Connections of Hope** in January, 2017. Nurses and pastors were oriented to the congregational nursing concept and to the structure, role and function of COH in the community. Opportunity was given to join, schedule training workshops and negotiate appointments with congregational nurses and church leaders.

Further recruitment is ongoing as presentations are made to spiritual communities about COH, as advertising in the media, and networking with groups and individuals.

II.   *Characteristics and Qualifications of the Congregational Nurse*

Following the call or inspiration to become a Congregational Nurse is expected, followed by professional considerations, such as:

1. Education and Experience
    - Be an active registered nurse with a current license
    - BSN degree is preferred, or a RN with leadership and current nursing skills or recent nursing experience, defined as having been within the last five years in the following areas:
      a. Emergency Department or Outpatient Clinics
      b. Ambulatory Care
      c. Medical/Surgical or Acute In-patient Care
      d. Home Health/Public Health/Hospice
      e. Nursing Education
      f. School Nursing/Occupational Nursing
      g. Mental Health Units/Clinics

2. Professional Attributes
    - Knowledge of health/healing ministry of the spiritual community in which he/she will serve
    - Knowledge of wholistic philosophy
    - Sensitivity to integrating and applying the spiritual aspects of wholistic health personally and professionally
    - Skill in listening and communicating therapeutically
  - Knowledge of health services and community resources or have willingness to learn about them

- Motivated to grow personally and professionally
- Knowledge of current nursing and health care issues
- Flexibility and ability to adjust to a varying schedule
- Ability to work autonomously and network

3. Competencies
   - Must have demonstrated nursing and health assessment skills
   - Must have organization and leadership skills
   - Must demonstrate the ability to analyze individual and group health care needs
   - Must have skill in organizing and supervising individuals and groups in activity and to work with highly diverse types of groups and individuals
   - Must be people oriented and enjoy working with groups as well as individuals using communication and motivational skills
   - Must possess skill in teaching and communication both orally and in written format
   - Must possess documentation skills related to health care and maintain accurate, clear records of activities
   - Internet-based technology skills a plus

4. Personal Characteristics
   - Have a relationship with God
   - Possess an empathetic personality along with well-developed diplomatic skills and a senses of responsibility and confidentiality
   - By psychologically and spiritually mature with a special desire and aptitude for pastoral ministry
   - Practice nursing using wholistic health care principles
   - Be politically adept and understand the importance of developing effective communication channels with leadership

III. **Liability Coverage**

Every practicing nurse is required to carry personal liability insurance coverage. Those who are retired should also carry liability insurance. Congregational Nurses who work with or participate in Connections of Hope programs and services must be covered. Professional group liability is provided by COH with a conservative benefit package.

IV. **Recruitment of Lay Volunteers & Job Description**

The **Connections of Hope** volunteer serves as an unpaid member of the caregivers' network in a variety of roles which reflect skill and experience. The Congregational Nurse may recruit, train, and give direction to volunteer activities. The Volunteer serves as a vital assistant to health promotion programs, office duties, and individual helping services.

1. *Recruitment Purpose and Process of Volunteers*

The **Connections of Hope** administers the lay volunteer Shepherd Center Ministry which provides both independent programs to the community and assistance to congregational nurses in their congregations. Established programs that serve the community in response to referrals are:

a. Wheels That Care (transportation to elders and disabled)
b. HandyPerson Assistance (domestic repairs, etc.)
c. Senior Walking Program (to increase mobility of elders)
d. Welcome Baby (monthly visitation to families with new babies for 1 year, providing a monthly milestone newsletter and offering assistance)
e. Friendly Visitor (acts of helping kindness to homebound and isolated
f. Managing a Small Income (financial education seminars)
g. In-home Respite Care

Community members may recommend certain skilled volunteers by means of a Recommendation Form (See Appendices, page Volunteers may be invited by community congregational nurses to participate with the use of a Volunteer Registration Form. **Connections of Hope** is notified and orientation or training by COH (or the congregational nurse if preferred) is arranged. COH encourages the establishment of the above programs in the congregations by their volunteers, then an agreement to provide volunteer services by the same in the surrounding community is encouraged in order to respond to referrals that come to the COH for individuals not connected to a congregation or in a congregation without a nurse program.

Connections of Hope also recruits volunteers in the community by other means to participate in these and other special programs so that community needs that COH is able to fill by its mission is made possible.

2. Coordination of Volunteer Services & Programs
Congregational Nurses recruit and coordinate volunteers in their congregations according to their goals and objectives and expressed need through assessments they make. COH requires that a monthly reporting of activities occurs and encourages that recruiting, coordination and supervision take place according to standards published by COH that assures safety and confidentiality of clients.

For needs the congregation is not able to fill, referral should be made to the COH office so that general community volunteers may be matched to respond. Congregational Nurses are encouraged to develop incentive and reward programs for volunteers on a regular basis that affirm their service and commitment. **Connections of Hope** through The Shepherd Center also conducts an annual recognition event for all volunteers.

3. Education and Experience of Volunteers
Education and experience are required for a few specific programs such as Managing   a Small Income and HandyPerson Assistance. Generally, all that is required is a sense   of service, care, and respect for individuals as a child of God. Training is provided for all volunteers which orients to the mission and purpose of COH and its programs and instructs in specific skills for visitation and personal assistance.

4. Personal Characteristics Required of Volunteers

- Have a personal relationship with God
- Be emotionally mature and practice sound judgment
- Be in good physical and mental health
- Accept instruction readily; possess ability to instruct others
- Be dependable and flexible with commitments and time
- Practice tact and compassion with others: congregational members and staff
- Have ability to project joy, encouragement, hope to others
- Be able to exercise patience; seek to understand
- Listen sympathetically without giving medical advice or making judgments concerning medical diagnosis or treatment

5. Accountability

The volunteer within the congregation is accountable to the congregational nurse and pastoral staff. Those working with the general community from the Shepherd Center are accountable to the Director of the Shepherd Center Ministry. The volunteer in either position is expected to:

- Meet regularly with and receive direction from the congregational Nurse
- Complete a monthly report of activities that is initialed by the Congregational Nurse and sent on to the **Connections of Hope**
- Preserve the confidentiality of clients served
- Assure the safety of clients served by following ethical guidelines and knowing the limitations of lay volunteer service as spelled out in training and supervision
- Report conditions observed that present a threat of well-being to clients served or volunteers to the Congregational Nurse or COH within 24 hours

Liability insurance coverage for volunteers is provided through **Connections of Hope** by a special program of Traveler's Insurance. Those who provide transportation and who drive to appointments on behalf of COH are required to have a valid driver's license and liability coverage on their automobile.

6. Working Conditions

Volunteers may work in homes of clients, community centers, public meeting hall, hospital, churches, offices, or outdoors depending on their activities. Those with mobility deficits may be assigned to sedentary work that greatly supports the organization. Those with identified skills are matched with complimentary needs or trained for other services.

Most programs and services require transportation.

7. Performance Evaluation

The congregational Nurse or the Administrator of **Connections of Hope** administers a performance evaluation on a 3-month basis to volunteers in their first year. The consultation in this activity provides opportunity for establishing satisfaction and fulfillment in the volunteering ministry and feedback to COH about the effectiveness of programs and services. After the first year, evaluations take place yearly. The Performance Evaluation for Volunteers may be found in the Appendix.

NOTE: Recommendation Form and Application are on the following pages.

Recommendation Form

Personnel of Connections of Health, PineTree Valley

Volunteer's Name _____ Age Group * _____ Position Sought _____

NOTE: Rate the performance qualities in this individual you observe from the left column in reference to volunteerism with this caregiving ministry. On the right underline or circle the description that best explains that performance quality. Make your Comments on the back.

Performance Quality: Excellent

Spiritual influence	❑	❑	❑	❑	❑	Dedicated, growing, searching, uncommitted
Spiritual commitment	❑	❑	❑	❑	❑	Active support, passive, acceptance, resistance
Attitudes	❑	❑	❑	❑	❑	Mature, adequate, inconsistent
Dependability	❑	❑	❑	❑	❑	Consistent, erratic, poor
Leadership potential	❑	❑	❑	❑	❑	Natural, latent, follower
Cooperation	❑	❑	❑	❑	❑	Consistent, erratic, poor, obstructive
Has Initiative, Resourcefulness	❑	❑	❑	❑	❑	Confident, imaginative, original, easily persevering, discouraged, lazy
Intellect	❑	❑	❑	❑	❑	Quick, average, slow to grasp
Personality	❑	❑	❑	❑	❑	Extroverted, well-balanced, ego-centric, unselfish, easily offended, accepts criticism
Adaptability	❑	❑	❑	❑	❑	Flexible, open-minded, prejudiced, rigid, tactful, out-spoken, blunt
Appearance	❑	❑	❑	❑	❑	Well-groomed, relatively neat, slovenly, careless
Emotional stability	❑	❑	❑	❑	❑	Stable, self-centered, easily disturbed, unstable

*Age Groups: teen, young adult (18-24 yrs), adult (25-54 yrs), older adult (55-64 yrs), elder 65+)

Your Name _____   Date _____

Volunteer Application

Date _____

Name _____ Phone _____ E-mail _____

Address _____City/town _____ Zip_____

Emergency Contact _____(Relationship)_____ Phone _____

Information needed for Criminal Record Check:

Date of birth _____ Sex: ❑ Male ❑ Female   Social Security # _____

Have you ever been arrested for a crime and/or incarcerated? ❑ Yes ❑   No

If so, please explain _____

Education:

Highest grade completed:

❑ High School ❑ GED ❑ Technical School ❑ College ❑ Post graduate

Course of Study _____ Degree _____

Other formal education and/or training _____

Professional certification _____

Volunteer skills you bring to this organization _____

Language(s) spoken _____ ❑ I have a valid driver's license ❑ Auto Insurance

Employment History: Please list your 3 last employers beginning with the present one.

Employer _____Position_____ Contact _____

Address _____ Phone _____

Employer _____Position_____ Contact _____

Address _____ Phone _____

Employer _____Position_____ Contact _____

Address _____ Phone _____

Previous Volunteer Experience:

A. Organization _____ Supervisor _____

Phone _____ Kind of work performed _____

B. Organization _____Supervisor _____

Phone _____ Kind of work performed _____

References: (Please do not include relatives)

A. Name _____Address _____Phone _____

B. Name _____Address _____Phone _____

150

Volunteer Application, cont'd . . .

C. Name _____ Address _____ Phone _____

What kinds of volunteer or career activities have been especially rewarding to you?

_____

_____

How much time can you give in volunteer service with COH? ____ weekly ___monthly

Days and Times you are available_____

 Why would you like to volunteer for COH? _____

_____

What would you like to get out of volunteering? _____

Statement of Agreement:

I am interested in serving as a volunteer. I am prepared to receive training and to devote the agreed-upon time to the purpose for at least one year. I will hold **Connections of Hope** blameless if I incur an injury incident during my work as a volunteer.

As a volunteer applicant, I understand **Connections of Hope** requires a criminal background check. I grant permission for such a check. I also give the organization staff permission to contact listed references. All information in this application form is accurate.

Applicant's Signature _____ Date _____

CHAPTER FOUR

Evaluation of CONNECTIONS OF HOPE

Careful, measurable records are kept of the quality of community agency relationships and collaboration shared, relationships of congregational nurses and volunteers of spiritual communities, and professional interventions with members of those communities through:

- Documentation of health education program offerings according to date, topic, attendance, demographics of attendees, other significant interaction, and observations of response in behavior change
- Documentation of interventions of home visits, assessments, and consultations
- Client satisfaction surveys
- Periodic health status research as follow-up to community health assessment of 2010
- Anecdotal reports from spiritual community leaders, health professionals, clients and families
- Reports of collaborating referral agencies
- Internal audit of congregational nurse and volunteer reporting
- Contracts with community entities

Objectives of evaluation are based on stated and observably measured improvement of health and quality of life of individuals. **Connections of Hope** desires outcomes that reflect effectiveness of its mission stated in Chapter One.

Results of evaluation will be reported yearly to agencies and individuals that fund **Connections of Hope** as well as to local community agencies that refer clients and express interest in involvement in the success of this organization. Reports will be available to the public.

Congregational Nurses are expected to perform evaluations on their activities in relationship to their congregations. Each will receive an annual report of **Connections of Hope** and will see the results of each contribution to promotion of health and quality of life.

Evaluation Form can be found in the Appendices.

APPENDICES TO OPERATIONS MANUAL

What Your Congregational Nurse Will and Will Not Do
(Example Handout--Amenable to Your Practice Policies)

Can and Will

•   **Answer general health questions** such as, "What I can do to make my disabled spouse safer and more comfortable?" "What will happen if I change the schedule of my medicines?"
•   **Visit you in the hospital or rehabilitation center** to help you understand your treatment plan and make a link to home, the church, and the community
•   **Help you understand your post-surgery/procedure instructions**, if you were still groggy from anesthetic when discharged from out-patient surgery.
•   **Reinforce teaching of self-care procedures**, such as testing your blood sugar.
•   **Help you get set up with various community agencies,** if you need some special services, like housekeeping aides, home nursing care, or support groups, or volunteer help
•   **Help you make a list of questions to ask and to understand medical procedures** when you or a loved one are receiving medical or critical health care
•   **Visit you in your home if you are unable to get out,** and provide routine health checks such as taking your blood pressure, checking your feet, listening to your lungs, discussing your needs and arranging for assistance
•   **Provide spiritual and social support to you in times of transition** – terminal illness, stress, marriage, divorce, birth, other difficult times.
•   **Organize and present health education programs and screenings** so you can understand your physical needs and changes and become more responsible for your own and your family's health
•   **Maintain your privacy.** Congregational health information will be reported to church committees only by categories and numbers

Will Not

•   **Give daily baths and other personal care.** However, your Congregational Nurse can instruct and supervise other caregivers in these activities.
•   **Prescribe or supply medication,** unless the nurse is a primary care provider
•   **Give injections or treatments.** However, for immunization campaigns, your Congregational Nurse can arrange to provide immunizations (such as flu shots) for recommended groups. Advanced Practice Nurses may provide a broader scope of care which might include medications, according to state regulations.
•   **Make health problems go away,** but will try to help you understand what is happening.

Connections of Hope

The Parish Nursing Service ◆ **The Shepherd Center Ministries**

123 Sunrise Drive, Anytown, U.S.A.

Wheels-That-Care GUIDELINES for RIDERS

The "Wheels That Care" transportation program of **The Shepherd's Center** began in October, 1990. Since then volunteer drivers have provided the means for older adults without resources to travel to doctor or clinic appointments or to do essential shopping. That service is expanded to include younger persons with disability and without other means of transportation. Other volunteer services are described in our brochure. To assure accountability and positive relations between volunteers and those receiving assistance, the following guidelines are established. Please read them carefully and, if in agreement, place your signature below.

1. When you are unable to find transportation to the doctor, clinic, grocery store, bank, or other necessary place, please call our office at XXX-XXXX between 9:00 am and 12:00 noon, Monday through Friday. If the office staff are unavailable, you may always leave a message on voice mail, which is checked periodically through the day. You can be assured that your message is heard and will be responded to.

2. Please call our office at least 48 hours in advance of the time of your appointment. Volunteer drivers must make time in their personal day to assist you.

3. Please DO NOT call the driver for your ride. We do not encourage giving riders the phone numbers of drivers. This office coordinates your service and provides the necessary insurance for it, so must make the contact with drivers.

4. We provide this service free; however, when possible, we encourage riders to contribute to the cost of fuel and upkeep of driver's vehicles by donating 45 cents/mile when possible.

5. We also encourage donations to **Connections of Hope** directly when possible. The existence of this non-profit organization is a community responsibility and appreciates your support.

If you wish to discuss how you may contribute in other ways with time or talents, please call us.

Your signature here demonstrates that you have read the above Guidelines and agree to receive services as described on the accompanying application.

Name _____Date _____

Connections of Hope

The Shepherd Center Lay Ministries
1123 Sunrise Drive, Anytown, U.S.A.

Wheels-That-Care GUIDELINES for Drivers

General Description of Program

The Wheels-That-Care program is a volunteer transportation ministry providing round trips for medical/dental reasons and for essential shopping or business. Special attention is given to matching the drivers with the special needs of the rider. The following guidelines are necessary to assure reliability to both driver and rider, efficiency, and confidentiality.

Validation and Accountability Guidelines

1. Drivers must present a valid driver's license and proof of active auto insurance* including liability and model of automobile to the Director of **Connections of Hope** for entry into agency records.

2. Completion of the application process, including receipt of references, and attendance at a 2-hour orientation session is required before volunteering begins.

3. Drivers are requested to provide a schedule of usual availability for volunteering.

4. Drivers are required to attend at least four (4) volunteer meetings with COH/year.

5. Drivers are expected to be available a minimum of one a month.

6. Drivers, as all other volunteers, are encouraged to agree to service with COH for at least one (1) year after acceptance of application.

7. Drivers are required to maintain a record of trips made including the following information:

Name of client	Date and Time of trip
Purpose of trip	Mileage

   Comments about any unusual circumstances

8. Drivers are requested to call in the report by Friday; leave a message if necessary.

9. Drivers are advised to not give personal phone numbers to riders.

10. Drivers must not accept calls directly from clients regarding need for transportation, but must receive coordination from COH. Advise clients to call the COH office if they happen to call you.

11. Please report any trips canceled to the COH office, giving the apparent reason for cancellation.

12. Clients who are able, are asked by COH to voluntarily contribute 33 cents/mile toward the use of the car to the driver. This volunteer service is extended to those without other available resources and pressure regarding payment is not to be applied. Funds will be sought for drivers who are not able to meet the expense of long-distance trips.

13. Donations beyond the cost of the trip are to be sent by the client to the COH office.

Service Guidelines

1. Drivers are asked to be alert to special needs of clients that COH or other agencies may respond to.

2. Drivers are asked to remain with the client at the doctor's office or while shopping and to assist the client into and out of the car (Pick-up trucks are not acceptable vehicles because most clients will have difficulty entering and leaving them.)

3. All drivers are required to attend the orientation sessions presenting safe physical assistance techniques and emergency measures yearly.

4. Drivers will be given the home phone number of the client and should call the day before appointment to make arrangements for the trip.

5. To preserve the privacy of clients, discussion with other community residents of your volunteer activities toward them is discouraged.

Thank you for joining our volunteer force. We anticipate a satisfying relationship together. May God bless our efforts.

----

* Connections of Hope provides additional, or excess, insurance with Nationwide Insurance Agency of America for all volunteers which covers auto accident and liability. It is imperative that COH knows about every trip made and the details mentioned above about reporting so that coverage may be accurately provided. If you desire details about the insurance plan, you may obtain them at orientation sessions and from the COH office.

JOB DESCRIPTION

Administrator, Connections of Hope

Position Summary: Administration of a 501 (c) (3) agency of professional health and lay human services ministries in a rural or urban community. Duties include program and service development; policy making; collaboration with and strengthening of community health and human service agencies and spiritual communities. It also includes providing a link for formal and informal services to enhance the health and quality of life in individuals of all ages in need. Other necessary duties are public relations, promotion, grant writing, and coordination of professional and lay activities. The Administrator is accountable to the Board of Directors of the Connections of Hope.

Qualifications: A strong candidate will have education and experience in community health issues and program development--desirably with a Master's Degree in Public Health Administrator or Public Health or Community Health Nursing. Skill in training and directing volunteers in service ministry supporting the health focus of the organization is a necessary strength. The candidate should be attracted to this position from a strong personal and spiritual commitment to wholistically search the need of people in the community and should demonstrate the ability to communicate easily and sensitively with individuals and groups. Leadership skills required are:

1. A sincere desire to serve God and people and the ability to communicate the vision of the organization's mission to others
2. An understanding of and respect for the various expressions of faith in the community
3. Ability to develop and maintain collaborative relationships with community health and human service agencies and political entities
4. Intuitiveness in identifying community needs and finding solutions through the mission of Connections of Hope and communicating the importance of COH in community affairs
5. Ability to develop, to manage, and to report on outcome-based progress of the agency
6. Ability to build curriculum for professional and lay volunteers related to its services
7. Ability to identify funding sources, initiate grant proposals, identify local means of support with the purpose of effecting sustainability
8. Ability to maintain a working relationship with the Board of Directors, the Advisory Council of COH, and any connected national organization.

Essential Functions:

1. Managing daily activities centered around recruitment of parish nurses, lay volunteers, and their congregations as participants
2. Serving on various boards and committees of community agencies; promotion of mission and function of COH; advocating for coordination of services and response to need
3. Planning educational opportunities and programming
4. Developing funding base and proposals to reach and maintain sustainability
5. Working with congregational leaders to establish nurse practices in their congregation
6. Managing record development, evaluation programming and services, and fiscal activity

EVALUATION – Congregational Nursing

The following priority list is adapted from one developed for Community Health Nursing to measure outcomes that are sensitive responses to nursing interventions through inquiry by focus groups and questionnaires among community health nurses in South Carolina. From it you may develop your evaluation tool using Likert Scale and Yes/No responses for subjective statements, data gathering from statistics for rates of change in morbidity/mortality and health behaviors, and health behavior change surveys or HRAs.
(Alexander, J. and Kroposki, M. (1999). "Outcomes for Community Health Nursing Practice," *Journal of Nursing Administration (29)* 5; 49-56)

From this priority list, a survey can be constructed in a database software program to record, tabulate, and analyze results.

CLIENT-FOCUSED CARE

Client's psychosocial components of care
While/After receiving care from a Congregational Health Nurse the:
- client communicates appropriately with nurse.
- client has skills to care for self.
- client has resources to care for self (housing, transportation, food, human assistance).
- client communicates appropriately with the family/primary care giver(s).
- client enjoys safe and caring relationship with household members/caregiver(s).
- family/primary care giver(s) are able to care for client independently.
- client is satisfied with current situation.
- client states understanding that an injury might result due to noncompliance.
- client is motivated to participate in activities.
- client is motivated to participate in daily care.
- client expresses an understanding of his/her physical problem/limitations.
- client demonstrates coping skills for stress.
- client demonstrates freedom from depression.
  - client has adequate financial resources.
  - client lives in safe, comfortable, adequately ventilated and heated dwelling.
  - client has adequate private living space.
  - client verbalizes signs and symptoms of exacerbation of his/her illness

Client's physiological components of care
While/After receiving care from a Congregational Health Nurse the:
  - Client demonstrates increased strength and endurance after participating in a home exercise program.

159

- Length of time between hospitalizations or nursing home admissions increases.
- Client has reached highest level of mobility.
- Client states he/she manages pain satisfactorily.
- Client describes adequate nutrition and fluid intake by self/caregiver.
- Client demonstrates ability to manage elimination.
- Client/caregiver(s) demonstrates ability to provide personal hygiene.
- Client demonstrates ability to manage pulmonary hygiene.
- Client exhibits healthy integumentary system.
- Client understands and participates in appropriate immunization program
- Client/caregiver demonstrate ability to manage medication regimen
- Client exhibits stable vital signs, blood sugar levels (circle all that apply)
- Client demonstrates ability to manage respiratory needs (asthma, COPD, etc.)
- Client demonstrates ability to operate and manage assistive devices/equipment.

Nursing intervention/implementation components of care
After/while receiving care from a Congregational Health Nurse the:
- nurse is aware of limitations of care due to availability of resources
- frequency of nursing visits is appropriate for client care.
- nurse ensures services/resources are available to the client.
- Nurse completes an appropriate assessment.
- nurse identifies goals/areas to jointly work with client.
- nurse has provided education that needs the client's needs.
- nurse considers the client's prior functioning.
- nurse makes appropriate referrals for care.
- nurse provides family-focused care.
- nurse uses collaborative community relationships for the benefit of the client.
- client applies health care/self-care skills learned

Environmental/community safety components of care
After/while receiving care from a Congregational Health Nurse the:
- Rate of infant mortality has decreased.
- Exposure to lead is minimized for small children.
- The incidence of fetal mortality has decreased.
- Rate of disease in the community has decreased.
- Client has not had an unplanned pregnancy.
- Client received immunizations appropriate for age.
- Client/caregiver(s) is in control of health outcomes.
- Client's exposure to environmental toxins at home is minimized.
- Abuse has ceased within the client's home environment.

CONGREGATION (AGGREGATE) FOCUSED CARE

As a result of a Congregational Nursing practice the population experiences:

- ❖ Consistent health promotion programming appropriate to population need
- ❖ Adequate and appropriate visitation of homebound and hospitalized members
- ❖ Increased attendance and participation at church services
- ❖ Increased knowledge among members of care for self, family, and others
- ❖ Engagement of adequate force of volunteers to assist other members through various programs of service
- ❖ Periodic assessment of needs among various population groups of membership
- ❖ Collaborative function of Health Committee/Cabinet, pastoral staff, and Congregational Nurse
- ❖ Participation in activities of other agencies and services in the community
- ❖ Safe environment
- ❖ Collaborative relationships with community primary care providers
- ❖ Sustainable funding for maintenance of practice and growth of services

CLIENT HISTORY & ASSESSMENT

Name _____ Age/BD _____ / _____ Phone _____

Address _____ Email _____

Referred by _____ Reason: _____

Social Support: Lives with _____, Relationship _____

Caregiver _____, Relationship _____

Family: Local _____

     Distant _____

Describe physical/emotional support _____

_____

_____

Expressed/observed needs _____

_____

_____

Spiritual History: Church _____ Pastor _____

Pattern of attendance _____ Parish Nurse _____

Expressed concerns _____
Observed needs _____

Medical History: Hgt. _____ Wt. _____ BP _____ P _____ R _____ T ____

Allergies: Drugs _____ Food _____ Envir. _____

Recent/Current illness _____

_____

_____

Surgical Hx _____

_____

Current meds:

Drug/Vitamin/OTC	Regimen	Reason Rx.
_____	_____	____
_____		
_____	_____	_____
_____	_____	____
_____		

Mobility:
❑ walks w/o assist   ❑ walks w/ human assist   ❑ cane   ❑ walker   ❑ w/c ❑ Doesn't walk

Other concerns _____

_____

Nutrition: ❑ prepares own meals ❑ MOW - freq. _____   ❑ caregiver prepares ❑ tube fdgs.

24-hr. Recall _____

_____

_____

Dentition: _____ Fluid intake hx. _____

Eval. of kitchen environment _____

_____

Systems Assessment:
Skin:
Lesions _____ Turgor _____ Color _____ Temp _____
        ❑ Smokeless tobacco, Pattern of use _____
Condition of oral tissues _____

Senses: Vision _____   Glasses/contacts _____   Hearing _____

Respiratory: Lung sds. R _____   L _____, Sputum _____
        Char. Of Resp. _____
        ❑ Smoker   Pattern of use _____
_____

Heart: Sds. _____   AP rate _____

      Qual._____

Other obsv. _____

Circulation: Periph. Pulses   LU _____   L_____

                               RU _____   RL

_____

           Extrem. Color _____ temp. _____ pain? _____ amputation ____

           Other obsv. _____

G.I.:   Elimination _____ Appetite _____

       Expressed concerns _____

       Abd.palpation/auscultation _____

       Other obsv. _____

Genito/urinary: Expressed concerns _____

      Bleeding _____ Incontinence _____

      Drainage device _____ Urine _____

Skeletal: Posture _____ Joints _____ Devices _____

      Pain _____ Exercise _____

Neurovascular: Sensorium _____

      Deficits _____

      Expressed concerns _____

Mental/emotional:

Observations_____

      Depression sxs. _____

      Coping ability _____

      Expressed concerns _____

Safety (self) Concerns: _____

_____

Safety of Environment:

Neighborhood _____Relationship to neighbors _____

Entry to home _____ Structure _____

Mobility in home _____

Utilities _____

Services _____

Other concerns _____

Transportation Concerns_____

Lifestyle Risks:
❑alcohol - type, freq._____   ❑ Drugs _____   ❑ Obesity _____ lbs.
❑ Inactivity   ❑ Social _____   ❑ Other _____

Stressors: ❑ Family _____
                 ❑ Financial _____
                 ❑ Occupational

Family Hx. ❑Cancer   ❑Heart Dis.   ❑ Diabetes   ❑ Stroke ❑ MH ❑ Obesity ❑

Alcohol/drugs

Uses computer and/or internet: ❑ Yes   ❑No

NOTES:

Made in the USA
Monee, IL
16 October 2021